COUNTRY ROADS
of WESTERN BC

A tugboat hauls a barge into the mouth of the Fraser River. The Steveston dock is a fine place to watch the sunset and the boat traffic.

From the Fraser Valley to the Islands

COUNTRY ROADS
of WESTERN BC

LIZ BRYAN

VANCOUVER · VICTORIA · CALGARY

For David

Heritage House Publishing Company Ltd.
www.heritagehouse.ca

LIBRARY AND ARCHIVES CANADA CATALOGUING IN PUBLICATION

Bryan, Liz
Country roads of western BC: from the Fraser Valley to the islands / Liz Bryan.

Issued also in electronic formats.
ISBN 978-1-926613-94-9

1. Rural roads—British Columbia—Lower Mainland—Guidebooks. 2. Rural roads—British Columbia—Vancouver Island—Guidebooks. 3. Automobile travel—British Columbia—Lower Mainland—Guidebooks. 4. Automobile travel—British Columbia—Vancouver Island—Guidebooks. 5. British Columbia—Guidebooks. I. Title.

FC3817.5.B78 2011   917.1104'5   C2011-902280-X

Editor: Karla Decker
Proofreader: Andrea Scott
Cover and book design: Jacqui Thomas
Maps: Jacqui Thomas
Photographs: Liz Bryan
Front cover: Sheringham Point Lighthouse, one of many along Vancouver Island's dangerous west coast.
Back cover: Bright fields of tulips on Seabird Island near Agassiz, in the Fraser Valley.
Opposite: Lavender harvest in the Cowichan Valley.

This book was produced using FSC-certified, acid-free paper, processed chlorine free and printed with vegetable-based inks.

Heritage House acknowledges the financial support for its publishing program from the Government of Canada through the Canada Book Fund (CBF), Canada Council for the Arts and the province of British Columbia through the British Columbia Arts Council and the Book Publishing Tax Credit.

Printed in Canada

British Columbia's mountainous coast, a wilderness maze of islands and inlets, has never been an easy land to tame. It is steep, rocky, thickly forested, rainy and cold. More than 200 years after Captain Cook's first landfall at one of the tiny coves fronting the Pacific, it is still mostly uninhabited. The First Nations built a successful way of life here on the edge, but European settlement came painfully, slowly and in many areas not at all. Most immigrants came from an agrarian background and were looking for farmland; the steep forested mountains along the coast, so difficult to access, had little to offer. It is easy to see why most of today's inhabitants crowd into the relatively flat and arable lands of the Coastal Trench—southwestern Vancouver Island and the Fraser Valley—where, ironically, today's burgeoning cities have commandeered much of the pioneer pasture land once so eagerly sought after.

The few small settlements along the rocky Pacific edge have a distinctly different character from those inland, built not on farming but on resource extraction. The isolated bays, inlets and fog-shrouded valleys are home to small fishing villages, lumber camps, mines and mill towns, always at the mercy of fluctuating supplies and world prices. Some have thrived; some have not. Increasingly, adventure tourism is stepping up to provide alternate incomes in this land where the prime commodity is wilderness.

Some of the country roads in this book lead through farm fields and orchards, particularly in the Fraser Valley, the largest pocket of arable land in the whole of British Columbia. (Despite encroaching suburbia, even around Vancouver and Victoria there are still roads quiet and pleasant enough for rewarding travel.) Roads farther flung exude a strong whiff of salt air as they explore rocky shorelines and beaches, fishing villages, coves and harbours and islands still adrift in worlds of their own. Old logging roads and railways, mining camps and whaling stations,

*Creamy surf rolls
in at Long Beach,
in the misty sunset.*

isolated First Nations villages, tiny ports—some reached only by sea or by dusty travel along rough forest tracks—have a more adventurous appeal than the quiet lanes of the Fraser Valley or the Saanich Peninsula. Then there are places that even today cannot be reached by any sort of road. Some of these are included in this book because of several little ships that carry freight and passengers through the maze of islands and down long inlets to reach them. On these sea lanes, you can discover some of B.C.'s most historic places and catch a sense of the true coastal wilderness. Whichever road you choose to travel, all the destinations are worthy of discovery. ❖

The Fraser Valley stretches in an alluring triangle 150 kilometres from its apex near Hope to the great river's three-fingered delta at Vancouver's southern edge. On a geological time scale, the valley is all new land—sediments 500 metres thick scoured by the river from the British Columbia heartland during tumultuous eons of land erosion, vulcanism and glaciation. The sediment filled what used to be an inlet of the sea, bounded by the Coast Mountain ranges to the north and the Cascade Mountains to the south. In all of B.C.'s deeply indented and fragmented coast, the valley is unique, the largest area of fertile arable land in the province. And thanks to a government policy of agricultural land preservation, it is still mostly an idyllic rural landscape, a mosaic of small farms that is divided east-west by the surge of the Fraser River. Though increasingly nibbled at the edges by expanding subdivisions, the valley offers worthwhile country road explorations.

The river was the valley's first transportation route, used by First Nations who lived along its banks and later by European miners boating upriver to the Interior goldfields. Steamboat landings along the way became the focus of later towns and villages. The first land track through the valley was slashed by Hudson's Bay Company fur traders, who followed a First Nation trail from White Rock beaches up the Nicomekl and Salmon rivers to the Fraser, where they later founded Fort Langley. Later trails were made by surveyors mapping Canada's boundary along the 49th parallel and by the Royal Engineers, who carved the first wagon road from New Westminster to Hope and the goldfields beyond. Later still, railway travel dominated the valley: first the Canadian Pacific and the Canadian National and then the feisty little B.C. Electric Interurban, which provided passenger service on its all-electric tramcars until the 1950s. Now the automobile era has taken over, and there are roads everywhere.

Above the yellow fields of daffodils around Bradner rise the snowy peaks of the Golden Ears, so named because of their golden hue at sunset.

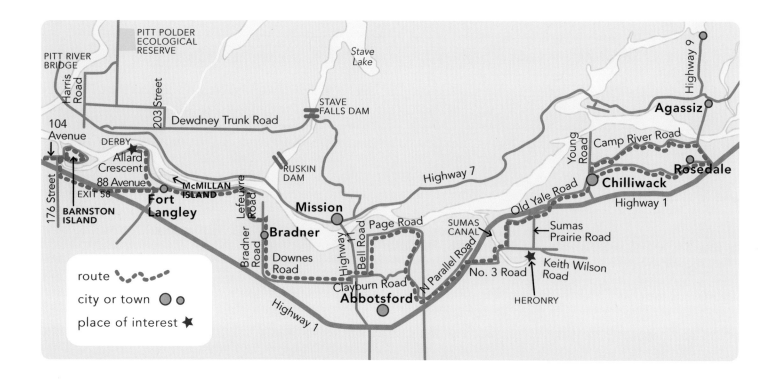

The Trans-Canada Highway dominates the valley, but this can be avoided. A great many smaller roads wind through the heart of farm country still embellished with old barns and pioneer houses, dairy pastures, orchards and vineyards, fields of berries and vegetables, farm markets, nature preserves—and a gentler, slower pace of life. And when one lifts one's gaze from the fields, there is always the beauty of the mountains. The highway drive from Vancouver to Chilliwack takes less than an hour; on country roads, the same journey could very well take all day, a day spent driving slowly and savouring the serenity.

Our first excursion begins with a visit to Barnston Island, a fat little crescent-shaped island, one of several beached in the lower Fraser. Amazingly, it still can only be reached by an odd little ferry: a barge, accommodating five or six cars, pushed by a tugboat. The service is free and runs on demand from 6 a.m. to almost midnight. (The residents apparently like the access the way it is, having voted down plans for a bridge.) Also amazingly, for land so close to a growing metropolis, the island is mostly farmland protected within the Agricultural Land Reserve: a wide-open country space laced with weedy drainage ditches and sprinkled with a few old barns and farmhouses, an organic beef farm, a herb-and-vegetable farm, two dairies, cranberry fields, cows, goats, sheep, ponies, and many hawks and eagles. Along the south shore, the small Katzie First Nation reserve accommodates homes and small docks for fishboats.

Devitt's farm barn is one of the few remaining pioneer structures left on Barnston Island.

Lying low in the river, the island farmland is shielded from floods by a high perimeter dyke. A 10-kilometre loop road on top of the dyke provides paved footing for winter walks, when the mountains across the river are ethereal with snow, and hoarfrost coats the wayside weeds. Spring is lovely, too, with young goats and lambs in the fields and dandelions thrusting up beside every ditch. The island has become a popular biking destination, especially for young families on sunny weekends. Whether you circumnavigate Barnston on foot, by bike or by car, it will be a pleasant excursion. To reach the island, drive east on the Trans-Canada from Vancouver and take 104 Avenue (Exit 50) north to the ferry landing, which is next to Surrey Bend Regional Park. Because of the peculiarities of the ferry, automobile traffic must back on and off the ramp on the island side of the crossing.

Barnston Island was named in 1827 for Hudson's Bay Company clerk George Barnston, who accompanied Factor James McMillan on his journey to found the trading post of Fort Langley, so it is appropriate that the fort is the next destination. Once off the ferry, turn south on 176 Street, join the highway heading east, and then take Exit 58 onto 88 Avenue, which is signposted for Fort Langley. Turn left (north) on Glover Road. The village that grew up around the fort has become almost a destination in itself, for it still holds many traces of its pioneer past, including vintage homes, two heritage churches, a large and shady Victorian graveyard, a magnificent community hall, antique shops, boutiques, restaurants and several museums. One of the museums is located in the 1915 Canadian National train station, which is surrounded by banks of peonies planted by the station master's wife. From the riverside parking lot of historic Jacob Haldi House (now the Bedford House restaurant), there is a fine view of McMillan Island and

11

the steepled 1897 church of the Holy Redeemer, situated on the Kwantlen First Nation reserve. Across the river, the snowy peaks of the Golden Ears really do turn golden in the sunset. Until 2009, a ferry crossing the Fraser here added to the antique ambience of the village but has since been replaced by a toll bridge downstream.

Before the establishment of Fort Victoria, the fort at Fort Langley (at the east end of Mavis Avenue) was the main Hudson's Bay Company coastal depot for furs and diplomatic dispatches, the nucleus for colonial trade, industry and settlement. Barrels of salted salmon and crates of cranberries found a ready market in the gold-mining camps of California. The fort is a historic park, and while only one log building is original, several others have been faithfully reconstructed. Stores, workshops and residences (including the two-storey Big House, where the crown colony of British Columbia was first proclaimed in 1858) are well stocked with authentic artifacts, and the fort's stockade and bastions have been partially rebuilt, complete with cannons.

In summer, interpreters in antique garb act as workers pressing stacks of furs, making barrels for salted salmon, manning the forge in the blacksmith's shop, spinning, weaving, serving behind the counter in the trading room and engaging in other pioneer pursuits. For a contemplative overlook, climb into a fort bastion, squint through one of the gun ports at the fields and river below, and imagine the wilderness that once lay all around and the isolation the traders must have felt so far from civilization.

The present fort, which dates from 1839, is not the first to be built here. Twelve years earlier, in response to urgent claims of American sovereignty over all the land known as the Oregon Territory, the Hudson's Bay Company, acting for the British Crown, sent the schooner *Cadboro* up the Fraser to establish the first trading post north of the Columbia River, delivering a strong political message that this was British land. They chose a site just downstream from the present one. This Fort Langley was later considered too small and inconvenient, and the company built a bigger and better one on higher ground a few kilometres east. Though the old fort was abandoned, the significance of the site, the first firmly held colonial outpost on the lower Fraser, was not lost to Governor James Douglas.

In 1858 he chose the riverside clearing for a settlement that he called Derby, after the British prime minister of the day. Groomed to be the future capital city of the new mainland Colony of British Columbia, the townsite was surveyed, and tenders went out for construction of a courthouse, a jail, a church and parsonage. The Royal Engineers under Colonel Moody were called in to establish military headquarters here. When Moody arrived, he quickly saw that Derby was totally unsuitable for a capital city: it was too far upstream and on the wrong side of the river to be defended against enemy (American) attack. The water here was also too shallow to accommodate seagoing ships. He countermanded the whole scheme and chose to build the new capital,

Queensborough (later New Westminster), nearer to the river's mouth.

By this time, Derby was already a going concern. The little church of St. John the Divine had been built—the parson, Reverend William Crickmer, ensconced in his parsonage, and the first service already celebrated. There was also, of course, a saloon, the What Cheer, run by Samuel Robertson and his wife, Julia, daughter of a Cowichan chief. Situated in a line of ramshackle buildings, it shows up quite clearly in a sketch of Derby's main street drawn by the Reverend Crickmer in 1859. The Robertsons later left the saloon business and became among the first to homestead at Albion on the north side of the Fraser, directly across from the fort. Some of the original cherry trees and grapevines they planted there still survive. Julia's beautiful white marble tombstone sits in shaded serenity in Fort Langley's cemetery, near St. Andrew's Church, which dates from 1885. The bell in St. Andrew's Gothic steeple is reputedly from the Hudson's Bay steamship, *Beaver*, which was built in England in 1835 and was the first steamship on the Pacific Coast to ply the Fraser River. History is interwoven here.

Derby townsite lingered for a while, but later all was abandoned. In 1881 the vacant church, made of sturdy California redwood, was barged across the river to the village of Maple Ridge, where it stands to this day. Nothing is left of the first Fort Langley or the town, but the site is preserved in Derby Reach Regional Park, a pleasantly rural swath of riverside property edged with split-rail fences and shaded by a stand of black cottonwoods, home to a colony of great blue herons. There's riverside camping and good fishing off the river bar. Across the road from the fort site stands Houston Farm, built in 1909 by Alexander Houston, the son of the more famous James Houston, who is credited with the first gold find on the Fraser River. The farm and its small frame house and huge barn are included in

13

a heritage property covering both the site of the first fort and some of the old Derby townsite. Walking trails loop through the land and along the riverbank. To reach this historical site, turn off Glover Road (the main Fort Langley village street) onto 96 Avenue, and drive west. Where the road takes a sharp left, go straight onto McKinnon Road, then turn right onto Allard Crescent and follow it to Derby Reach.

To continue the journey, leave Fort Langley by River Road, which skirts under the fort's stockade to follow the river (although the high-banked track of the CN Railway pretty well hides the river from view for several kilometres). Prominent to the north are the twin peaks of Golden Ears, and, to the south, blueberry and cranberry fields occupy the boggy flats. About five kilometres along, past several river-side enterprises, including the Fort Langley float-plane base, River Road jogs north to the pioneer community of Glen Valley. Here, anchoring the corner of Glen Valley Regional Park, the red-painted heritage Hassall House (1917) is typical of early pioneer homes built beside the river. There's good fishing on nearby Two Bit and Poplar bars.

River Road eventually peters out, but before it does, drive up the slopes of Pemberton Hill via Lefeuvre Road onto the benchland that

Early pioneers built their homes beside the Fraser, relying on river-boats for supplies. This is the heritage Hassall House at Glen Valley.

During the Bradner Daffodil Festival, local growers showcase their wares in the local community hall.

has proved most favourable for growing daffodils. A British settler with the odd name of Fenwick Fatkin imported some bulbs from Holland in 1914 and started a flower farm in the Bradner area, primarily to grow daffodils. His success in the field spurred other farmers to plant the bulbs, and today, at the peak of the mid-April growing season, the community holds a long-weekend daffodil festival. Fields in the area turn to vivid gold, and every driveway, it seems, sports a flower stand. It's a glorious time of year. Keep on Lefeuvre to McTavish, then drive east onto Bradner Road. North of this intersection, beside the CN rail tracks, lies Bradner's old store and gas station, and north again is the Jubilee Hall. If it's festival time, head south to the community hall beside the school, where the flower show has taken place every year since 1928. Here, hundreds of different varieties of daffodils are on display, and growers stand by to take orders for fall bulb delivery. Volunteers serve lunches and daffodil teas, and a craft fair is usually taking place. Ask where the best fields of daffodils are (try Haverman Road), and search for that quintessential view: a field of daffodils with snowy Mount Baker or Golden Ears in the background.

Continue south on Bradner Road until just before it ducks under the highway. Turn left (east) here onto Downes Road, a hilly little thoroughfare that rides north of the highway, passing several farm markets and garden stores. Keep going to the very end (about nine kilometres), then turn north onto Seldon Road, which leads to Clayburn Road at a traffic-controlled intersection on Highway 11, south of the Mission Bridge. On Clayburn Road, cross the highway and continue on to Clayburn, the earliest company town in B.C., founded in 1905 by Charles Maclure to house the workers at his Clayburn Brick Works.

A large deposit of fireclay on nearby Sumas Mountain provided material for the bricks that were shipped to towns and cities across Canada. While the factory has since moved to more modern premises nearer to Abbotsford, Clayburn remains a small rural village, with a quaint, almost old-English flavour. Along its flower-filled lanes are a dozen old company homes, including five foremans' cottages (made of Clayburn brick, of course), a heritage school and a church. Its heart is the two-storey red-brick general store, nicely renovated and still very much in business, partly as an old-fashioned English sweet shop and Yorkshire deli, partly as a traditional country tea room. Across the street is a playing field where one can well imagine a game of cricket underway. The tiny village, a rural enclave almost within the growing sprawl of Abbotsford, is worth a saunter. Most of the buildings were designed by the brick factory owner's brother, Samuel Maclure, who built Tudor Revival mansions for the rich and famous in early Vancouver and Victoria and was one of B.C.'s premier pioneer architects.

Clayburn General Store, the focus of attention in this first company town in B.C., shares its huge interior with an old-fashioned sweet shop, deli and tea house.

After enjoying a pot of tea, when you're ready to leave this little bit of old England, return west along Clayburn Road a few blocks to Bell Road, drive north through the fields, cross the railway tracks, turn right onto Page Road and continue east until it seems you can go no farther. Here by the Fraser's edge is the beginning (or end) of the riverside Matsqui Trail; ahead lies an unpaved road that climbs over Sumas Mountain, providing superb views north across Fraser River farmland to the snowy thrust of Mount Judge Howie in the Coast Mountains. The road is used to haul rock from the old Clayburn quarry, so drive extra carefully. Sumas Mountain Road winds down again into the valley to meet Straiton Road (which leads more directly from Clayburn Village and is a way to avoid the mountain drive for the faint of heart or those with tender vehicles). Keep going down through the old communities of Straiton and Kilgard until the road meets Highway 1. Go east on North Parallel beside the highway to Number 3 Road (Exit 104) and cross to the south side. In spring, there are usually fields of daffodils in this part of the valley, and it's always worth stopping at The Yellow Barn for fresh country produce.

Keep on Number 3 Road, turn north on Boundary Road and east on Keith Wilson Road to cross the Vedder Canal, built back in the 1920s as part of a huge drainage scheme. This

The ethereal snows of the Coast Range hover above this idyllic Fraser Valley dairy farm.

part of the valley was once inundated by a shallow lake fed by a Fraser backwater and spring high-water overflow from the Chilliwack and Vedder rivers. The canal and an assortment of dykes, ditches and pumping stations drained the lake, and farmers moved onto the land. In 1948 extreme high water breached the Sumas dyke and the land was drowned once again. Evidence of this flood can still be seen on various old buildings in the area. The settlement of Sumas had its name changed to Greendale in 1951 to avoid confusion with Sumas, Washington.

A few blocks farther east on Keith Wilson Road, 130 hectares of flood plain at the foot of Sumas Prairie Road have been set aside as the Great Blue Heron Nature Reserve. You can get information and a map of the reserve trails at the Interpretive Centre. The heronry itself, more than 200 nests bunched high in the cottonwoods, is best seen through binoculars from the dyke path or via a webcam set up in the centre. There is always plenty of action during the peak nesting season in April. Other birds to look for include many species of waterfowl, eagles and hawks, and a veritable choir of songbirds. Western painted turtles live in the slough and hoist themselves out onto logs to bask in the sunshine.

From the heronry, return to the Vedder Canal bridge and drive north onto Chadsey Road, which leads onto Old Yale Road, a section of the earliest east-west route through the Fraser Valley. A little way east, at the intersection with Adams Road, stop to see Sumas Methodist church, an old-timer (1886) now renovated and serving as a wedding chapel and photography studio. To keep on Old Yale Road (now Highway 1A), cross the highway at the Lickman Road overpass, veer right and continue east through busy urban Chilliwack. Though some parts of it are not rural, Old Yale Road is worth driving for its historically significant, well-marked heritage sites along the

way. It follows the meanders of Hope Slough, where several First Nations villages were once located, and passes through the settlements of Cheam (1871) and Rosedale (1875). Rosedale still has the feel of an old village, with its church and other buildings clustered around a bend in the road. Nearby is the ballpark, established in 1910. Here Old Yale Road leaves Hope Slough and heads east to meet Highway 9, which connects Highway 1 with Agassiz and Harrison Hot Springs on the north side of the river (see Chapter 4). For a break in the journey, the floral displays of Minter Gardens are almost directly on your path, a short drive south on Bunker Road. Or, cross the highway and drive east to the quiet woodlands around Bridal Veil Falls, a cascade most aptly named.

Holstein cows cluster in the doorway of a milking shed near Camp River Road.

The return loop to Chilliwack, however, requires a short drive north on Highway 9 and then a turn down Ferry Road, on your right just before the bridge. This road ducks under the bridge approach and leads west past the long-gone ferry dock and a shingle beach before turning onto Camp River Road, a beautifully rustic pioneer route that follows the serpentine passage of Camp Slough. At one point, the road becomes a shady lane overhung with giant maples draped with ferns and moss. There are interesting barns, a few pioneer homes, goats and dairy cows, tree farms, a rhododendron garden and nurseries—and stupendous views south across the fields to Mount Cheam and other peaks in the Lucky Four Group of the Cascade Mountains.

North toward the Fraser, the land is a patchwork of islands carved by meandering creeks and sloughs: Fairfield Island, Hog Island, Rose Island, Windermere Island and Rosebank Island, all traversed by a maze of farm roads, some of them connected by old bridges. It's an area well worth exploring. Just past Rose Island, Camp Slough ambles north to join the Fraser, and the road follows Hope River, which leads west all the way to Young Road, one of Chilliwack's major north-south routes. At the north end of Young Road is the site of Minto Landing, where a ferry used to cross the river to the CPR station at Harrison Mills (the landing was named after one of the early sternwheelers on the river). The ferry service enabled Chilliwack farmers to send their produce by train to market at New Westminster. Near the old ferry landing, at a site not commemorated in any way, Simon Fraser is said to have landed on his epic journey to the sea in 1808.

Young Road leads south back into Chilliwack, now one of the largest cities in the Fraser Valley. Here, the Trans-Canada Highway is easily accessible for the return journey to Vancouver. ❧

TRACKING THE BORDERLINE

One of the most interesting drives through the Fraser Valley follows the 49th parallel east from Boundary Bay almost to Hope, where the flat valley lands bump up against the ramparts of the Cascade Mountains. It's a route unobstructed by major settlements and unhampered by traffic lights, and it is slow enough to allow plenty of time to consider why the border is where it is, and how it was ever made.

Boundaries between nations are usually decided by geographical features—a height of land, a lakeshore or the meanders of a river—features that people can see and respect (or fight over). The Canada/U.S. border follows a straight line that exists, like other lines of latitude, only on paper or in the imagination. It has been described as "topographically absurd," a description that seems supremely apt as one sees it on a map, knifing across ridges and rivers and keeping its purity of direction even across the steepest mountains.

The Oregon Treaty of 1846 chose the 49th parallel as a compromise solution between the land claims of the British Colonial Office (which modestly wanted all the old Hudson's Bay Company fur lands north of the Columbia River) and the United States (which thought that its territory should stretch to Alaska). A joint Boundary Commission was empowered, and survey parties from both governments were to be sent out to establish this compromise boundary line using astronomical observations and working with chains and compasses.

Eleven years after the Treaty was signed (political decisions take time to implement), a workforce of 56 Royal Engineers, plus numerous hired axemen, packers, mule drivers and camp helpers, arrived from Britain to begin the job of marking the 49th parallel through B.C. to the Rockies. A comparable workforce started in the U.S. south of the line. Difficult enough, the job was hampered by the sheer rawness of the land. There were no roads or railways; the valley

The 49th parallel strides true to its course over the rugged Cascade Mountains. Often the cutline through the trees is the only boundary marker.

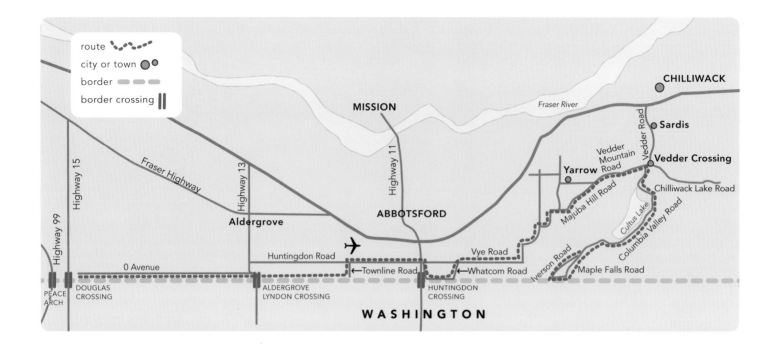

bottoms were thickly forested and marshy, teeming with mosquitoes; the mountains were steep and almost unassailable. Before surveyors could begin, trees had to be felled, supply roads hacked out though swamps and mountain valleys, roaring rivers bridged, camps set up and supplies organized. It was a monumental undertaking, particularly since the line, once both sides had agreed on its accuracy, had to be marked by iron obelisks sent from England, to act as mile markers.

Despite the enormous scope of the task, the boundary cutline between B.C. and Washington State was finished in two years, and today one can drive alongside most of it, at least where it traverses the flatlands of the Fraser Valley. West of Yarrow, Vedder Mountain stamps down its huge high foot, and the 49th goes ruler-straight over the top of it and down, then up again into the misty reaches of the high Cascades through Manning Park. (For further insights into the project, a good read is *Mapping the Frontier: Charles Wilson's Diary of the Survey of the 49th Parallel, 1858–1862*, edited by George Stanley and published by Macmillan.)

A day's country drive follows the boundary line almost as far as Hope, and adds a couple of side trips to other border points. Begin the trek at the Douglas Border Crossing just east of the Peace Arch. Access this from Highway 99 by taking exit 2A to Campbell River Road and turning south on Pacific Highway 15. Just before the customs building, turn east along 1 Avenue, then follow it around to 0 Avenue, which sits just north of the 49th parallel, probably in no man's land, the seven-metre swath that divides the nations. For much of its way east, the boundary line consists of little more than a ditch and/or a fence—and sometimes nothing at all—between fields

and shrubbery that look much the same north and south.

The road, of course, is straight, if hilly in places, but it cannot be called dull. Remote, peaceful and lovely, this stretch of the valley is worth driving at any time of year: spring dandelions and daffodils give way to summer buttercups and cow parsley, the pale stars of thimbleberries, glimmering moon-daisies, fields of strawberries and raspberries, then fall colours set against snowy peaks. The road is popular for family bike rides, and during the work week it is used as a commuter shortcut, but by and large you will have the road to yourself as you count the boundary monuments— yes, many are still there, where they were placed during the arduous work of surveying so many years ago, though some have been replaced with modern, skinnier versions and others can be hard to find in the bushes. Look for sturdy silver-painted obelisks sitting on the Canadian side of the line. Each is numbered for the miles from boundary Monument Number 1 at Point Roberts.

A lovely old weathered barn, its paint fading to soft grey, still stands right beside 0 Road, facing the Canada–US boundary line.

An undefended border indeed: a frayed barbed-wire fence defines the borderline west of the Huntingdon Crossing, marked by one of the official monuments.

Just after Monument 19, 0 Avenue (also known as Boundary Road) reaches the Aldergrove/ Lyndon border crossing. Simply follow the road as it angles around, crosses the customs lineup on Highway 13 and resumes its eastward thrust. A deep ditch here marks the line, and across it, the valley to the south opens up to views of Mount Baker. Near here, photogenic old homesteads and dairy barns nestle on both sides of the border. Near Monument 21, neat rows of raspberry bushes converge on the horizon. Today, this fertile land ranks with the most expensive farmland in Canada, but in the 1920s, it could be bought for less than $30 an acre. Bradner Road is worth noting: in April, dazzling daffodil fields and the locally famous Daffodil Festival and Flower Show in Bradner Hall are well worth a detour (see Chapter 1).

A little farther, at Townline Road, Boundary Road comes to an abrupt stop, mostly because the northern tip of Judson Lake pokes up from Washington State, forming a natural barrier and a site well known to birdwatchers for its concentrations of migrating waterfowl—and also because it is the only place in B.C. and Washington where the little blue heron has been spotted. If you stand at the corner of Townline and Boundary roads and look east, you can see the border cut, marked by a fence line, as it strides toward the lake.

Drive north on Townline Road through raspberry fields and packing plants toward Clearbrook, "The Raspberry Capital of Canada." Turn east on Huntingdon Road, from here the closest through road north of the border, and drive through the small community of South Poplar, where the cemetery is shaded by a "fence" of giant cedars. There's another monument, Number 30, at the south foot of McCallum Road, where the boundary is defined only by a tumbled wire fence. All of the dead-end side roads south along here are worth driving, if only for the scenery and

the farm-gate fruit, eggs, corn and other homegrown valley foods.

Continue east on Huntingdon then drive south on Highway 11 and head for the Huntingdon border crossing. Turn east on 2nd Avenue, which angles onto Boundary Road, back on the 49th parallel. After Boundary Road crosses the Sumas River, the boundary line climbs straight up onto the shoulders of Vedder Mountain, and travellers wishing to continue the borderline quest must find other roads. Boundary Road turns onto Whatcom Road, a continuation of the Whatcom Trail, a route that U.S. miners travelled to reach the gold claims on the Fraser and beyond. It was near here that the Royal Engineers set up their major Sumas depot—one small log house—and began their boundary survey, pushing both east across the mountains and west toward the sea.

Between the borderline and the Fraser River, the valley here used to be covered by a huge shallow lake with looking-glass reflections of the mountains all around. Surveyor Charles Wilson wrote in his diary,

A high waterfall cascades into the Klesilkwa River by the road leading south to the Skagit Valley. Mossy stream banks are starred with summer daisies.

Not many old farm buildings remain along 0 Road, but this one is well worth a photo stop.

"It is the most beautiful place I was ever in," but beauty wasn't everything. From mid-June until September, the marshy swamps around Sumas Lake were a breeding ground for mosquitoes. His diary continues: "The mosquitoes have now regularly set in. It is a perfect agony performing even the regular actions of life. Washing is perfect torture, they settle en masse upon you, perfectly covering every portion of the body exposed. We sit wrapped in leather with gloves on and bags round our heads and even that cannot keep them off; none of us have had any sleep for the last two nights." Some of the men suffered from malaria, and mules were blinded by the insect bites.

The whole valley bottom south of Chilliwack was subject to yearly floods when Sumas Lake, fed by a backwater of the Fraser, became the catch basin for spring run-off from the mountains. Pioneer settlers kept their distance, and roads were forced into long detours. Old Yale Road, the first wagon road through the valley from New Westminster, made a looping track south of Sumas Lake on its way to Hope and Yale, finding dry footing around the edge of Vedder Mountain. Later, the B.C. Electric Railway was also forced south of the lake on a high embankment. It wasn't until 1920 that the federal government dyked the rivers and drained the lake as part of a massive flood-control program. Vedder Canal was cut to lead water back into the Fraser, and eventually the lake bed became dry enough for settlement. Even so, many of the pioneer farmers chose to build on slightly higher knolls, a decision that protected them when the serious floods of 1948 breached the dykes and swamped the land once again.

East of the Huntingdon Crossing, stay on winding Whatcom Road north through dairy farm country to Vye Road, which parallels the high railway embankment. Drive east on Vye to Lamson Road, which ducks under the railway heading south. Take this road until just before it dead-ends near the border, then continue east on Maher Road, which becomes part of Old Yale Road. Where the road turns north, there's a good view of the borderline cut climbing up the steep forested slope of Vedder Ridge. From here, staying as close to the border as possible requires a zigzag route: east on Vye to Powerhouse, north to Wells Line Road, east to Inter-Provincial, north to Campbell, east to Town—a route that perhaps is close to the original Old Yale Road as it strove to keep its feet dry.

At the south end of Powerhouse Road there is indeed a powerhouse: a white concrete structure embellished with a classical Greek pediment bearing the name of the British Columbia Electric Railway Co. and the words "Sumas Substation." The top windows under the pediment are circular, like portholes. This substation powered B.C. Electric's Interurban railway, which ran between Chilliwack and New Westminster taking farm produce to market on its daily milk run, as well as carrying the mail and providing four round trips a day for passengers—an electric commuter line way ahead of its time. Instrumental in opening up the valley to farm settlement, the railway's passenger service ran from 1910 to 1950, when it was made redundant by the Trans-Canada Highway. It remains open as a freight line (no longer electric, it uses diesel engines), and its track, therefore, survives. The Fraser Valley Heritage Railway Society, whose long-term goal is to restore and operate heritage electric interurban cars on the full length of the original rail route, has acquired and refitted some of the early railcars and restored one heritage station, at Sullivan in Surrey, where it parks its rolling stock.

Town Road meets Boundary Road at the foot of the mountains and heads north to join Yarrow Central, the main street of Yarrow, a pioneer village settled by Mennonites in the 1920s and named by railway officials for the masses of wild yarrow flowers growing here when it planted its station. As a more dramatic alternative to Town Road, Majuba Hill Road turns uphill (right) off Town Road and extends for four kilometres along the ridge, providing good views through trees of the valley below. One of the few places in this area guaranteed to stay dry, the Majuba Hill plateau, named for a famous Boer War battle, was settled early. The first post office in the area—and the first school—was established here in the home of William and Mary Chadsey in 1900. Majuba Hill Road descends to the valley, and where it crosses the railway tracks at the bottom of the hill, a cairn in tiny Majuba Park commemorates the building of the first wagon road to Yale. Drive north to Yarrow Road, then turn right onto Vedder Mountain Road.

The steep blue bulk of Mount Cheam looms above Fraser Valley fields, where a wandering side road attracts scavenging crows.

Because of the mountainous nature of the border terrain east of here, there are no more stretches of a sedate Boundary Road from which to track the 49th parallel. But a couple of roads do meet the boundary, and each makes an interesting side trip. The first leads into the quietly rural Columbia Valley at the head of Cultus Lake—the site of a British Boundary Survey camp, and today a well-established summer recreation area. Almost surrounded by provincial parkland, the small communities of Cultus Lake and Lindell Beach and the camps and cabins along the shore are all within easy reach of wild forests and mountains.

Columbia Valley Road leads south from Vedder Mountain Road along the east side of Cultus Lake. At a prominent junction, take Iverson Road, which leads southwest directly to the border, where it joins Henderson Road (in essence another 0 Road) for a short stretch of borderline travel, complete with a prominent boundary marker. From this location at the end of the valley, one can see the border slash slicing up through the mountain forests in both directions, most clearly after a fresh snowfall.

The valley is divided by two major roads: Columbia Valley Road and Maple Falls Road. Both aim south toward their erstwhile destinations in Washington State: Columbia Valley Road led to Columbia, and Maple Falls Road led to the old town of Maple Falls, once a boisterous logging and mining community south of Washington's Silver Lake. This was an important supply centre for Columbia Valley settlers, some of whom, before a major re-survey in 1905, believed they were living in the U.S. (The road to Vedder Crossing was not put through until 1916.) Today both valley roads dead-end at the border, and this isolation gives the valley a unique charm. It is ruggedly rural, with tree nurseries, berry farms, a winery, miniature horses and a pig farm. There are some splendid split-cedar pioneer barns dating from 1900. All have cedar shake roofs and follow the same design: haylofts above, with milking parlours along the side walls (the first settlers in the valley were dairy farmers).

Return to Cultus Lake after your explorations and make your way back to Vedder Crossing, an important transportation hub when Yale Road was the only major thoroughfare to and from coastal

cities. The bridge at Vedder Crossing marks the start of the road leading south to Chilliwack Lake, a route used by Boundary Commission workers to access the border in the high Cascade Mountains. North of the Vedder Bridge is Camp Chilliwack, formerly a Canadian military engineers' training camp. While the camp is now closed and the land has been turned into a residential enclave, there is a very good military museum here, with all sorts of mementoes of the Royal Engineers, who surveyed the border, built most of the roads and plotted many of the pioneer towns and cities in British Columbia's early days. Farther along, on the outskirts of Sardis, is the site of Edenbank Creamery, western Canada's first cheese factory and the first farm to ship milk and cream to Vancouver on the B.C. Electric Railway in 1911.

The only other accessible section of the International Boundary lies at the south end of the Skagit Valley, near Hope. One can drive there quickly on Highway 1, but there are more leisurely alternatives. Follow Vedder Road north, turn right on Promontory Road then left onto Chilliwack River Road, one of the old winding pioneer trails. Just before Highway 1, turn right onto Prairie Central Road, a civilized country route that runs east through pretty farmland with some fine views of the mountains to the north. The road joins Annis Road, which leads onto the highway. Drive east toward Hope, then take Exit 168 to the Old Highway 1. Turn south along Silver-Skagit Road, which leads 60 kilometres to Ross Lake and, again, the 49th parallel. The road is paved for the first 10 kilometres to Silver Lake Provincial Park. Beyond, it reverts to good gravel, climbs a low pass, tracks the lively Klesilkwa River down into Skagit Valley Provincial Park and crosses the Skagit River on the 26 Mile Bridge.

Pinkish-red rhododendrons are among B.C.'s protected wildflowers. Drivers can see a small pocket of them along Highway 3 through Manning Park, but they are plentiful in the Skagit Valley.

The Skagit River rises in alpine Manning Park and runs at first generally southwest, then, joined by the Klesilkwa, it continues across the Washington border through the Ross Lake reservoir and a series of dams to flow leisurely into Puget Sound. Formed by glaciers that scoured its U-shaped bottomlands, the Skagit Valley is wedged between mountain peaks high enough to escape glaciation. Surrounded by their sharp towering spires and pinnacles, the valley offers appealing wilderness scenery despite a century of logging. Today it is a wildlife haven and prime recreational land for hiking, climbing, canoeing and fishing. Climatically benign, it enjoys a mix of coastal wet and inland dry vegetation, with average temperatures above those of the Fraser Valley and considerably less precipitation, due to a rain-shadow effect.

The valley is perhaps best known botanically for its displays of wild red rhododendrons. Motorists along Highway 3 through Manning Park catch a glimpse of their glory in a roadside park beside the Skagit River at Rhododendron Flats, but in late June and early July, the Skagit Valley provides riotous displays. The wild shrubs are found only in the Cascade Mountains of B.C. and Washington.

Before dams were built along the river, the Skagit Valley provided a relatively easy transportation route from the Washington coast near Bellingham to the goldfields of B.C.'s Interior, and in 1858, Captain Walter de Lacy of the U.S. army laid out a riverside cross-border trail that followed the Skagit and the Snass rivers to meet the old fur-brigade route and the Dewdney Trail (now retraced by B.C.'s Highway 3). A well-preserved 16-kilometre section of this track links the Skagit Valley here with Sumallo Grove, a lovely little park of giant cedars along Highway 3. An energetic day hike, the trail leads through the Skagit's steep, unlogged upper valley and past some of B.C.'s big relic trees: groves of giant cedars, tall black cottonwoods and ponderosa pines.

Discovery of placer gold brought an influx of mining hopefuls into the Skagit Valley around the turn of the century, and later, a couple of scam artists from Nevada salted claims around Shawatum Mountain so successfully that they sparked a stampede—and even the growth of an ephemeral mining town called Steamboat—before their larceny was discovered. Some pioneers tried ranching, but by and large it was logging territory, and much of the flat valley floor is now bushy second-growth.

In Washington State, the Skagit River has long been dammed to provide hydroelectric power for the city of Seattle. Between 1937 and 1949, the Gorge and Diablo dams were built, and later, Ross Dam was added to the system, backing up the river to form the 37-kilometre-long reservoir known as Ross Lake. A later raising of the dam caused Ross Lake to spill into Canada. Plans for further dam construction in the 1960s would have enlarged the lake even farther north, right up to the Klesilkwa River at 26 Mile Bridge. Stalled for years by the B.C. government and very active citizen protest groups on both sides of the border, plans for the High Ross Dam were eventually shelved. In 1996 the area became a provincial park, and, presumably, the valley is now safe from further encroachment.

The Silver-Skagit Road is primarily a scenic riverside and mountain valley drive, with several river access points and trailhead parking places for those hiking mountain trails or enjoying meadow walks. The river is one of B.C.'s best trout-fishing streams, and several meadows, including the sites of Whitworth and Chittenden, two pioneer ranches, display profusions of wildflowers in spring and summer. Birds and other wildlife abound.

Just north of the 49th parallel, Ross Lake Park provides lakeside camping, and farther along, the International Point picnic and boat-launch area, almost smack dab on the border, provide a good view (doubled by its reflection) of the western boundary slash. East, a rough scramble up onto a bluff leads to a boundary marker, the completion point of the first stage of the Boundary Survey from Point Roberts to the Upper Skagit in 1858. There is no border crossing here, but Silver-Skagit Road continues south for about two kilometres into Washington State, ending at North Cascades National Park's Hozameen Campground. Perhaps in the spirit of this border trek, one could opt to boat or swim the line of the 49th parallel across Ross Lake, but a picnic lunch along the shore might well suffice. ❧

3   FRASER FRINGE

Vancouver is wedged between Burrard Inlet and the Fraser River's great delta, and while the advancing suburbs continue to encroach upon much of the land around the city, some country roads linger along the river's edges, where much of B.C.'s early industries flourished. The route suggested in this chapter is necessarily broken by the river itself and by major highways, and some of it goes through built-up industrial and residential areas. But it leads to places interesting enough as destinations in themselves. And, taken as a whole, it is proof that breathing space and a country ambience still exist even around burgeoning Vancouver.

The route begins on Highway 99 south of the Oak Street Bridge, which spans the Fraser River's North Arm. The big island to the southwest is Sea Island, commandeered today by Vancouver International Airport. Heading south, take the first exit after crossing the bridge (Sea Island Way, formerly the route to the airport), then turn right on No. 3 Road and almost immediately right again onto River Road. River Road runs along the north shore of Lulu Island, which lies snugly between the North and Middle arms of the river. River Road ducks under Dinsmore and No. 2 Road bridges, cutting around the Richmond Olympic Oval, which sits between the bridges. It continues to the northwest point of Lulu Island, Terra Nova Park. Captain George Vancouver stopped near here in June of 1792 and bartered with local Coast Salish fishermen for several giant sturgeon weighing more than 100 kilograms apiece. The offshore area became known thereafter as Sturgeon Bank.

Settled in the late 1880s by Newfoundlanders who bestowed its name, Terra Nova later became the site of a fish cannery that operated intermittently from 1897 until 1928. The buildings were demolished, but the pilings can still be seen in the marshy tidelands north of the first parking lot. From here, enjoy the view across the river to the airport, the low blue hulk

In the dawn's pale light, a jaunty tugboat steams to sea down the Fraser's North Arm. Ruined pilings nearby mark the site of the old Celtic Shipyards.

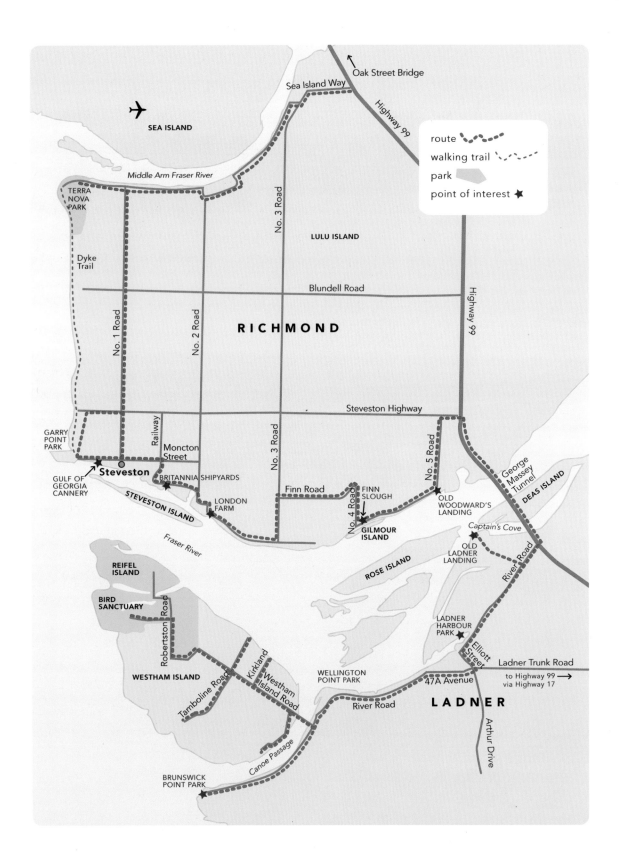

SEA ISLAND

Oak Street Bridge

Sea Island Way

Highway 99

Middle Arm Fraser River

TERRA NOVA PARK

Dyke Trail

No. 3 Road

LULU ISLAND

Blundell Road

No. 1 Road

No. 2 Road

RICHMOND

Highway 99

route

walking trail

park

point of interest ★

Steveston Highway

GARRY POINT PARK

Railway

No. 3 Road

No. 5 Road

Moncton Street

Steveston

GULF OF GEORGIA CANNERY

BRITANNIA SHIPYARDS

LONDON FARM

Finn Road

No. 4 Road

FINN SLOUGH

OLD WOODWARD'S LANDING

George Massey Tunnel

DEAS ISLAND

STEVESTON ISLAND

Fraser River

GILMOUR ISLAND

Captain's Cove

OLD LADNER LANDING

River Road

REIFEL ISLAND

ROSE ISLAND

BIRD SANCTUARY

Robertston Road

LADNER HARBOUR PARK

Elliott Street

WESTHAM ISLAND

Kirkland Road

Westham Island Road

WELLINGTON POINT PARK

47A Avenue

Ladner Trunk Road

to Highway 99 →
via Highway 17

Tamboline Road

River Road

LADNER

Arthur Drive

Canoe Passage

BRUNSWICK POINT PARK

34

of Point Grey and the shining peaks of the Tantalus Range, at the head of Howe Sound. Terra Nova Park, with its network of trails and several wildlife viewing areas, encompasses more than the shoreline. In addition to an extensive natural area, where the landscape is gradually being returned to its native state, a dedicated rural area with five pioneer homesteads, a farm centre and community gardens seeks to preserve Richmond's farm heritage.

One of the three original Newfoundland settlers, Joshua Parson (who came here to help construct the cannery), built a small gingerbread-style house in 1886 near the end of River Road. Still standing, it is being restored along with its heritage orchard and vegetable gardens. It can be seen from the dyke access road. A trail atop the dyke above extensive salt marshes on the seaward side continues south all the way to the village of Steveston. The land side of the dyke mostly provides a view of Richmond homes, except for a few fields around the original Steves family farm, whose cows are still sent out to browse on the salt marsh grass.

To continue on the route, head back east along River Road to No. 1 Road and then go south through residential streets to Steveston Highway. Turn west here and head for the dyke access, turning south again on 7 Avenue to reach Garry Point Park on the island's tip. Favoured by steady offshore breezes, it's a great place for flying kites and watching sunsets and ships, including large ocean-going freighters, on the Fraser's South Arm, its main channel. Back in 1827, when the SS *Cadboro* sailed upriver bringing Hudson's Bay Company traders to their chosen site of Fort Langley, the ship's captain named this point after Nicholas Garry, an HBC governor. Later, a lightship was stationed here to guide fishboats into the river, and in 1889 another short-lived cannery operation was established, reached from Steveston by a wooden boardwalk along the edge of a narrow slough known as Scotch Pond. The cannery and the boardwalk are gone, but Scotch Pond is still a very photogenic boat moorage. At the tip of Garry Point, a tall stainless steel net-mending needle commemorates local fishermen who lost their lives at sea, and a traditional garden commemorates the Japanese families who settled here, among them some famous boat builders. In May the unmowed park grass is blue with lupines.

From Garry Point Park, take Moncton Street to the renovated Gulf of Georgia Cannery, now a National Historic Site. A tour here is memorable: the interior is cavernous, and the place is stuffed with old equipment and vintage photographs. The site of present-day Steveston was bought in 1878 by William Steeves (the second "e" was later dropped). William and his father, Manoah, imported a herd of Holstein cows from Oregon and started a dairy farm, but ultimately it was fish, not farm produce, that fired the economy. Fishing fleets prospered, and by the 1900s, 14 salmon canneries were in operation. Steveston became a town, at one time claiming to be bigger than Vancouver. It had an opera house, a theatre and several hotels, houses and businesses, and provided steady employment on the fishboats and in the canneries.

Sunset from the Steveston wharf reflects gold off the fishboats and lends a rosy hue to distant Mount Baker.

But in 1918, fire destroyed most of the wooden buildings in the townsite, and the impetus for urban development was lost.

This could be seen as fortunate, for Steveston today is still very much a colourful fishing village, home to the largest commercial fishing fleet in Canada. Six hundred seiners, trollers and gillnetters line the wharves along Bayview Street, and visitors can enjoy it all from the riverside boardwalks. Moncton, the main shopping street, has kept and enhanced its turn-of-the-century nautical charms, though today most of the stores are stocked for tourists rather than fishermen. The historic Steveston Hotel, with its Buck & Ear Bar & Grill, is still very much open for business, but the old post office has become a museum. Also of interest is a restored Interurban railcar, built in 1913, which made the run on the B.C. Electric Railway to Vancouver for 45 years before the service ceased in 1958. Steveston has become a justifiably popular venue for weekenders out to buy fresh fish from the wharf, enjoy seafood at a riverside restaurant or take a tour boat out to the jetty to see the California sea lions, or farther, to watch whales. The pier itself is a good place for sunsets. Looking upriver, one can see the snows of Mount Baker turn rosy orange as the sun slips behind the hills of Vancouver Island.

Leave Steveston centre, driving east on Moncton to Railway Avenue; turn right, then right again at the school playground, heading toward the river to another National Historic Site, Britannia Shipyards on Westwater Drive. This is an outstanding restoration of a turn-of-the-century fishing community, well interpreted in a riverfront park where historic wooden vessels are moored along Cannery Channel. A dozen old waterfront buildings stand here, including the

oldest shipyard in B.C., dating from 1885. Four restored houses are built on stilts over tidewater, and a large Chinese bunkhouse shows living conditions between 1910 and 1930. At one time, 1,000 Chinese inhabitants lived and worked in the Steveston area, and opium dens flourished openly until the substance was declared illegal. The Japanese presence is documented by the faithfully restored Murakami House and Boat Works, which offer a time capsule of family life on the river.

From the shipyards, continue east on Dyke Road. Offshore lays the bushy shoulder of Steveston Island, created by dredging river gravels onto a long sandbar. Today it's a wildlife refuge, critical habitat for nesting waterfowl and bald eagles. A short distance east is Gilbert Beach and a public fishing pier. Nearby, historic London Farm provides yet more heritage interest. Settled by teenaged brothers Charles and William London, who arrived from Ontario in 1877, the farm became a self-sufficient community. The Londons ran a general store and post office and built a wharf where they brought in supplies and shipped out their farm produce—milk, hay and vegetables—to markets in New Westminster.

The wharf served, too, as a stopping place for boats from Victoria carrying goods and passengers upriver to the Fraser Valley. The elegant Victorian farmhouse was built by Charles in 1888 for his Scottish bride, Henrietta Dalziel. Six rooms have been restored and furnished in period style, and there is a cozy English tea room. The grounds are particularly noteworthy, planted with lawns and heritage flowers—lots of old roses—chosen to bring year-round colour. Behind the house sits the old Spragg family barn, a collection of antique farming equipment,

allotments (mini-garden plots) leased to locals, chicken houses and beehives. A walk around here, followed by a good cup of tea and a scone, provides a welcome respite. London Farm is usually open on weekends, and more frequently in summer.

Continue the drive upriver along Dyke Road to where it comes to a temporary end at the foot of No. 3 Road. Drive north along No. 3 through a part of Lulu Island still amazingly pastoral, with fields of broccoli and strawberries and a few old barns. Take Finn Road east to No. 4 Road, then drive south to connect with Dyke Road again opposite Gilmour Island.

If you like your history restored, cleaned up and interpreted, perhaps Finn Slough might not suit you. It's one of the last tidal communities on the West Coast and likely the very last small fishing village on the Fraser. Along both sides of the slough that separates Lulu Island from Gilmour Island are the old houses, net lofts and boat sheds of a salty maritime community founded in the early 1900s by immigrants from Finland. Living by the rise and fall of the tides, the fishermen built their homes on stilts or on floats along the shore and tied up their boats right alongside. When the tide is high, Finn Slough is a lustrous, though narrow, waterway and boats can slip in and out, but at low tide, the slough becomes a marsh of eelgrass and brambles, and boats are keeled high and dry at jaunty angles.

A wooden footbridge (the centre portion can be lifted to allow maritime passage) gives the 50 residents access to their island homes, and while this bridge is privately owned, no one seems to mind visitors crossing over and walking the short boardwalk trails on the island. Many of the buildings and docks are old, picturesque and somewhat time-worn artifacts of a long-gone age. Some are brightly painted and adorned with fishing floats, pots of geraniums and fishing

The picturesque decay of Finn Slough, the sole remaining independent fishing village on the lower Fraser, attracts photographers and curious travellers. Across the slough, these little cottages are still neat and trim.

Ladner Harbour Park is worth a visit, if only to see the boats. Across the river, these old cannery buildings attract the eye.

memorabilia. One bears a sign that reads Dinnerplate Island School. Near the bridge sits one of the last authentic blue-stone tanks where linen gillnets were soaked in a copper sulphate solution to prevent rot. Today's gillnets, often seen laid out to dry on the docks here, are made of nylon.

Good views of the slough, with its old boats and crooked buildings, can be had from the foreshore, especially near the slough's mouth and from the bridge. But naturalists, photographers and the just plain curious—who should take care not to invade residents' privacy—will enjoy a brief stroll on the island. As the rest of Richmond's Lulu Island becomes suburban, can Finn Slough survive? The ownership of the land, and the continued existence of this unique and historic village, is in question.

From Finn Slough, continue east along Dyke Road to No. 5 Road and the old Woodward's Landing site. Before the construction of the Massey Tunnel under the Fraser, a car ferry crossed the river here from Woodward's to Ladner's Landing on the south bank. Today the 1874 Woodward's community, with its small boat-building enterprise, a wharf and an inn for travellers, has been lost to light industry.

The route south now becomes circuitous, because the only way to cross the river here is by the George Massey Tunnel and also because one must drive through the built-up area of Ladner. Drive north up No. 5 Road to Steveston Highway, and turn onto Highway 99 for the trip through the tunnel. Take the first right turn on a small exit road marked River Road, then turn right on Ferry Road and drive through the Ladner Marshes to where Captain's Cove Marina sits near the old ferry dock. The land west of River Road here is covered by a flood plain forest and a freshwater tidal marsh, part of the South Arm Marshes Wildlife Management area, a haven for all kinds of

Westham Island is an agricultural delight, full of old barns and fields of berries and, in fall, migrating flocks of geese. The Bissett family homestead is next to the popular Westham Island Estate Winery.

wildlife and an important feeding ground for great blue herons. Near the marina, a short board-walk trail and viewing platform is perfect for birdwatching. Short trails also lead into this marsh from Ladner Harbour Park, a little farther south. It's worth the short drive in to the harbour if only to see the boats, the bright red two-storey wharfinger's office and the view across the water to photogenic cannery buildings by the old Government Wharf in downtown Ladner.

Continue south on River Road through Ladner to Elliott Street. Turn right here to see the old Ladner waterfront (Chisholm Street), but left to continue the drive. Turn right on 47A Avenue, which becomes River Road again. Follow the river dyke around the right-angled bend at Wellington Point Park, with its fishing pier and good delta views, then across the century-old one-way humpbacked wooden bridge over Canoe Passage onto Westham Island, at the very mouth of the Fraser's South Arm.

Most visitors make a beeline down Westham Island to the George C. Reifel Migratory Bird Sanctuary, located at the river mouth. But the island merits further exploration. Flat and richly fertile, here are the tidy farms and old barns, fields of cows, and hedgerows of blackberry bushes that speak of a bucolic country life, as far from crowded suburbia as one could wish. The first farm on the right is Westham Island Herb Farm, part of the larger Ellis Farm, a family enterprise started in 1916 to grow grain and hay for horse-logging teams on Vancouver Island. The sacks of feed were put directly onto boats from the farm landing at the end of Kirkland Road. Today, the farm specializes in berries and vegetables, 20 varieties of pumpkin and squash, and 6 different kinds of potatoes, as well as cut flowers and honey, and, of course, fresh herbs. For U-pick strawberries, follow the Ellis Farm U-pick sign. There are several lovely old buildings here, including a century-old barn.

The longest side road is Tamboline Road, which meanders southwest. Along here in 1885, Joseph Tamboline arrived from Italy, started a small grain and hay enterprise, then turned to dairy farming. The farm has been in the family ever since, and now, as Emma Lea Farms, specializes in fresh vegetables and all kinds of berries, including strawberries and blueberries. With its small farm store and ice-cream parlour, Emma Lea Farms is a popular summer destination. Also along Tamboline Road is Westham Island Apiary, which sells eight different varieties of honey, including dandelion. Farther along, Westham Island Road turns right onto Robertson Road and crosses onto Reifel Island. Just before the bridge is Bissett Farms—notice the fine old blue-painted house— and the adjacent Westham Island Estate Winery.

Close to federal and provincial wildlife reserves on adjacent Reifel Island, the fields of Westham Island attract vast flocks of snow geese on their migrations from Siberia.

Take a few moments to drive or walk on these farm roads, enjoying the country ambience before switching into birdwatching mode at Reifel Island, a place to experience the wonder of migration as 1.5 million birds wing their way in and out during spring and fall. Its marshland, ponds and canals provide nesting and feeding havens for birds of all kinds, from geese to hummingbirds—240 species in all. Its tall trees are nesting sites for raptors, eagles, owls and herons. When 30,000 snow geese arrive in fall to settle on the fields and mud flats for the winter, one could well imagine a vast and undulating snowdrift has arrived from Siberia. The refuge is well known to Vancouver birdwatchers and popular on sunny weekends, when families arrive to feed the ducks on the ponds and stroll along the trails.

To end the trip on a reflective note after your island experience, return across the bridge to the mainland and continue south along River Road to Brunswick Point Park. Here you can stroll to the very tip of land that divides the river from the ocean and watch the sunset over the ghostly ruined pilings of the once-thriving 1897 Brunswick Cannery.

To return to Vancouver from here, make your way back along River Road to Ladner and take Ladner Trunk Road east to Highway 17 (the road to the Tsawwassen ferry terminal) for access to Highway 99. ❧

4

NORTH RIVER TO HOPE

The first settlements along the Fraser River's north bank were steamboat landings, supply points for the rush of miners heading upstream to Harrison or Yale, where the overland gold-rush trails started. Some gold seekers stopped their quest and decided instead to carve out homesteads beside the river. The landings soon became shipping centres, where goods came in and forest and farm products went out to markets in New Westminster and Victoria. When the Canadian Pacific Railway was completed north of the river in 1886, landings such as Haney, Whonnock, Silverdale, Mission and Deroche became stations, and the railway supplanted the river as the valley's lifeline. It wasn't until the early 1900s that the great surveyor Edgar Dewdney and his team of Royal Engineers surveyed Dewdney Trunk Road, which is named after him. It was built along the north side from Port Moody to Deroche and cut well away from the river to provide access to pioneer farm settlements. Until its replacement by the Lougheed Highway (now Highway 7) in the 1930s, the trunk road was the chief artery north of the river.

Dewdney Trunk Road is still an important thoroughfare through the packed suburbs of Pitt Meadows and Maple Ridge, and it makes a good start to a journey along the less-travelled north side of the Fraser. At the Pitt River Bridge, Highway 7 angles southwest to follow the river, while the Trunk Road keeps straight east. While this first stretch is by no means a country road, it does provide access to a fascinating rural area known as the Pitt Polder. A *polder* is the Dutch word for land reclaimed from the sea, and Dutch farmers were the first to settle here to reclaim land from the Pitt River marshes by means of a series of canals and dykes. The area, with its small fields and dairy farms, is still reminiscent of Holland, though most of the land has reverted to marsh and is now preserved in a Wildlife Management Area. To visit this excellent birdwatching spot, turn north from Highway 7 onto Harris Road and cross the Alouette River.

Seabird Island's spring tulip festival is held when its fields of tulips are in brilliant silky bloom under the looming shoulders of Mount Cheam.

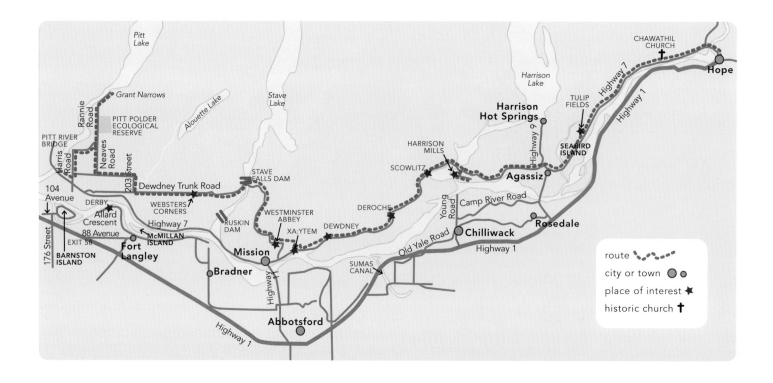

Harris Road connects to Rennie Road, which leads along the Pitt River to the Grant Narrows boat launch at the south end of Pitt Lake.

Trails along the network of river and marshland dykes, and several high towers and platforms, provide good viewing of the large variety of birds that nest or visit here, including greater sandhill cranes and tundra swans. An important rest stop on the Pacific Flyway, the marshes host hundreds of thousands of geese and ducks on their migratory journeys, and osprey, eagles, hawks and herons at any time of year. Beaver, muskrat, frogs and other aquatic creatures also live here. Nature lovers are lucky to have such a rich wilderness reserve so close to a metropolis. If you take the time for a quick visit, go early in the morning and keep your binoculars handy.

Dewdney Trunk Road can be reached from Harris Road, but it changes into a succession of avenues as it skirts between the wandering Alouette River and the urban sprawl that has engulfed the old villages of Pitt Meadows, Haney and Maple Ridge. Turn south along 203 Street to reach Dewdney Trunk Road again. Despite the urban nature of the road here, traces of the pioneer past linger on. Laity Farm in Maple Ridge was established in 1879 and is still family-owned. Known locally for its pumpkin patch and petting zoo, the farm has a fine old house and barn, both built in 1912. The nearby Hampton Farm dates from the same era. St. John the Divine, one of B.C.'s earliest churches, was built across the river in 1858 in the short-lived townsite of Derby, near Fort Langley (see Chapter 1). Partially dismantled, it was hauled on scows

Eternally snowy, Mount Baker in Washington State dominates the central Fraser Valley near Mission, where the river is still a major shipping corridor.

across the river and rebuilt in 1882 at the corner of today's River Road and Laity Street. Haney House on 224 Street dates back to 1878 and has been restored and refurbished in period style. Afternoon tea is served on the veranda in July and August.

North of Haney lie connecting roads into popular beaches and campgrounds on Alouette Lake in Golden Ears Provincial Park, a huge swath of high mountain wilderness that adjoins Garibaldi Provincial Park and stretches beyond Whistler. It is named for the prominent double peaks of the Golden Ears, a valley landmark that has given its name to a new highway bridge crossing the Fraser nearby.

Dewdney Trunk Road continues east into more rural areas. The crossroads community of Websters Corners still retains some country ambience with its two false-front commercial buildings and general store dating from 1932. James Webster was the first European to come here in 1882 and cut down the forest to make farmland. By 1891, the community was big enough to warrant a post office. A group of Finnish families arrived here from the disbanded commune on Sointula Island in 1905 (see Chapter 12), and their leader, Matti Kurikka, started a cedar-shingle mill nearby. Several Finnish-style homes, some still with their separate traditional saunas, survive from this era and so, too, does the large Sampo Hall, the cultural heart of the Finnish community, built by volunteers in 1915.

At Websters Corners crossroads, 256 Street leads south to Kanaka Creek Regional Park, in an area first settled by Hawaiians (or Kanakas) in the employ of the Hudson's Bay Company at Fort Langley across the river. The densely forested park stretches 11 kilometres along the creek right down to the Fraser's shore and includes two very impressive waterfalls and a slick, natural waterslide worn into the rock by the rushing cascades.

Dewdney Trunk Road passes the entrance to the University of B.C.'s Malcolm Knapp Research Forest and Rolley Lake Provincial Park, then jogs north and rides along the very top of the Stave Falls Dam, completed in 1912. There are two dams here: Stave Falls, which backs up the river to form the Stave Lake reservoir, and Ruskin Dam, built 1929, which spans a granite gorge six kilometres downstream to create the Hayward Lake reservoir. B.C. Hydro maintains a visitor and interpretation centre at the upper dam site, where one can view the turbines and generators of this working museum and stroll or picnic on the grounds.

Dewdney Trunk Road crosses Stave Falls Dam and leads east to Steelhead, another old community. Here the road bends south, heading toward the river, but it veers east again to bypass Mission town centre. This former riverboat settlement once had dreams of greatness. Optimism started when members of the Oblate brotherhood founded St. Mary's Mission and Residential School here in 1861; it grew when the Canadian Pacific Railway arrived in 1885, called the station Mission and helped start the townsite. Lots were auctioned off in the "Great Land Sale" of 1891. Later, the Burlington Northern Railway chugged north from Washington, bridging the Fraser (for a long while, this was the only river crossing in the valley) to provide the first rail connection to Seattle. To accommodate later automobile traffic on the bridge, planks were laid between the rails. Mission swiftly became the industrial and commercial centre of the valley: the world's largest supplier of cedar shakes, the strawberry capital of B.C., site of two major fruit canneries/ jam factories and home to the Eddy Match Company, the largest match factory in the world, which closed only in the 1960s. For many years, Mission hosted a famous Soapbox Derby. But bust followed boom; railways and roads were built south of the river, and towns such as Abbotsford and Chilliwack eventually eclipsed Mission. The floods of 1948 wiped out the strawberry and other berry fields, supplies of cedar dwindled, the Soapbox Derby was superannuated, and the buildings of St. Mary's Mission and school were demolished in 1965.

Today, a new road bridge and improved commuter rail service has perked interest in the town, and it has become almost a bedroom community for Vancouver. The downtown area, however, keeps the feel of an English market street with a string of small individual shops and several heritage buildings. The mission site is now within Fraser River Heritage Park, on a bluff overlooking the river at the eastern edge of town. All that remains of the mission community here is the church bell, cast in 1875 and now atop a new bell tower, the Oblate cemetery, and a building constructed in 1961 that is now a trade school and a training centre for First Nations police. The extensive grounds, with their masses of rhododendrons and roses, are well maintained, providing a centre for local fairs and festivals, including yearly pilgrimages to the

reconstructed Grotto of Our Lady of Lourdes, with its onion-domed chapel. The park Visitor Centre, known for its Blackberry Kitchen Café, is situated in a pioneer house.

West along the river from Mission is the small community of Silverdale, settled by Italian immigrants in 1880 but more famous as the site where notorious train robber Bill Miner held up and robbed a CPR mail train back in 1904.

Leaving Mission, return to Dewdney Trunk Road and drive east through a rural area north of town to a lane, just east of the intersection with Stave Lake Road, which leads up to Westminster Abbey. High on the shoulder of Mount Mary Ann, the abbey and its separate, high bell tower dominate the skyline, even from across the river. This is one of only two Benedictine monasteries in Canada. Construction began here in 1954, but the church itself was not completed until 1982. Designed by architect Asbjorn Gathe, the church is neo-Gothic, shaped in the form of a Greek cross, with a central altar. Inside its somewhat dour, angular concrete exterior, under the upsweep of a wonderfully fluted and vaulted ceiling, 64 brilliant stained glass windows bring in explosions of light and colour. It's a powerful place, equal to any of the great cathedrals of Europe. The grounds are manicured, the surroundings very rural, the views sublime. And when the 10 bells in the tower ring out, a sweet sense of serenity settles over the meadows. The monastic abbey is also a seminary, and the community of 30 monks is almost self-sufficient: their farm supplies most of their meat and fresh produce. Visitors are always welcome to walk in the gardens, but the magnificent church is open only on Wednesday and Sunday afternoons.

Past the turnoff to the abbey, Dewdney Trunk Road turns south, wriggles through the neighbourhood of Hatzic and comes to an end at Highway 7, which rides roughshod over the old route. But east from here, Highway 7 is a pleasant two-lane, often winding, road all the way to Hope. Immediately east of the junction is Xa:ytem/Hatzic Rock National Historic Site, where an ancient First Nation village was likely deserted when most of its inhabitants were wiped out by smallpox in the 1800s. Almost two hundred years later, developers clearing land for a new subdivision around an odd-shaped prominent rock bulldozed up so many ancient stone tools that they had to call in archaeologists. They found traces of a 5,000-year-old pit/plank house whose 128 post holes showed that the dwelling had been remodelled several times. Carbon-14 dating of artifacts found on the site pushed the date of area occupation back to 9,000 years ago. In the oral history of the local Sto:lo, the large odd-shaped rock is a powerful transformer where three chiefs who challenged the orders of the Creator were turned to stone. Their life force persists in the rock, which has always been a First Nation sacred site. To help interpret the locale and the legends, the Sto:lo people have built a longhouse, a boat-building shed and two pit houses. Visitors can participate here in interactive programs and workshops for Salish weaving, drum making and other traditional pursuits and, of course, visit the sacred transformer stone.

Dewdney Trunk Road (now merged with Highway 7, or Lougheed Highway) goes east to Dewdney (also named for the surveyor). This old settlement has an interesting general store that was once a busy hotel. Just east of the Dewdney Bridge, Hawkins Pickle Road (who could resist exploring here?) leads to Inch Creek Hatchery, where coho, chinook, chum and steelhead are incubated and released. Of particular interest is the large, dark pond that is home to several huge white sturgeon, monster fish that have remained unchanged since the Jurassic period, around 65 million years ago. One of the fish here weighs more than 90 kilograms. Once plentiful, Fraser River sturgeon are protected: they can be fished only on a catch-and-release basis.

Between Dewdney and Deroche, a pioneer settlement named for Joseph Deroche, who arrived from California in 1860, both Highway 7 and the CP railway cut across Nicomen Island, the first of several islands cut off from the mainland by backwater channels or sloughs that edge the river here. Just before Nicomen Slough Bridge, River Road leads leisurely toward the Fraser, past a popular pub, a wild-berry winery and wharves. At the end of this road is Dewdney Nature Regional Park, where boats can be launched to explore the river and the network of sloughs, just as local First Nations did in their dugout canoes. Nicomen Slough's quiet waters provide passage for salmon en route to spawning grounds along neighbouring creeks, and this annual migration attracts hundreds of bald eagles. The slough also provides winter habitat for trumpeter and tundra swans. For those in search of pastoral scenery, Nicomen Island Trunk Road loops south from the highway through farm fields; a short spur leads to the river's edge at old Deroche Landing.

Harrison Mills was once a flourishing pioneer village, but today the sole relic is Kilby Store and Farm, now a historic site still stocked with pioneer sundries. Seen from the Harrison River dyke, it seems enfolded in greenery.

Scowlitz is a First Nation community on the banks of Harrison Bay, a widening of the Harrison River just before it empties into the Fraser. This is another very ancient place. Near the Harrison mouth, at a site known as Qithyll, archaeologists have excavated a 2,000-year-old village site of pit/plank houses built in a row and showing evidence of continuous habitation for centuries before abandonment. Behind the village terrace lie an amazing number of earth mounds and rock cairns, known locally as the Scowlitz Mounds or the Fraser Valley Pyramids. Several of these have been investigated. The largest one, a rectangular cairn three metres high surrounded by concentric rings of boulders, is thought to be the burial site of a chief. He was interred with a trove of grave goods, including copper discs and rings, abalone shell pendants and roughly 7,000 beads made from dentalium shells. Many more mounds and cairns—a total of 198 of them in 15 distinct clusters—lie along the slopes of Harrison Knob. At present, there is no public access to these ancient cemetery sites, which are on private reserve land.

The land around the mouth of the Harrison River, inhabited for so long by First Nations, is also one of the most historic places in B.C. from a European settlement point of view, although scant traces remain. Industry came first in the form of a fish-packing plant: the Hudson's Bay Company opened a station here to salt-pack salmon into barrels for export. It became a supply depot back in the tumultuous days of the gold rush, when miners left the Fraser here and headed up the Harrison River, the start of the earliest route to the goldfields of the Cariboo. When the Cariboo Wagon Road was cut through the Fraser Canyon north from Fort Yale in 1862, this route slipped into obscurity, and the river mouth became a minor refuelling point for wood-burning paddlewheel steamers. Then, in 1886, the CPR drove west along the Fraser's north bank from Hope to the coast. Settlement began anew around the station at Harrison Mills. Passengers and freight for the railway came from local lumber mills and by ferry across the river from Chilliwack. Harrison Mills became an energetic pioneer town with a school, mill workers' houses, a store and a boarding house.

It was a short-lived heyday: the lumber mills declined and/or burned, and other railways on the south side of the Fraser diluted the traffic flow. The town was virtually deserted, but one store and farmhouse stubbornly remained. Owned and run by the Kilby family, it was a tall sprawling structure housing the local post office, a general store, a hotel, and the family's living quarters, all connected by a ramp to the railway station on the embankment across the road. When the first automobiles appeared in the valley, the Kilbys added gravity-fed gas pumps (which remain today). They also ran a farm, as most pioneers had to do, for fresh supplies of milk, eggs, meat and produce. Today, Kilby Store and Farm has been refurbished as a B.C. Historic Site, kept much the way it looked in the early years of the 20th century. Pioneer nostalgia is strong here as one strolls around the farm and the well-stocked store, peeks into hotel bedrooms or walks down the leafy lane to the riverfront park. In summer, interpreters in period costume add to the antique mood. To reach the Kilby site from Highway 7, look for School Road just east of the Harrison Bridge, drive south, and then turn west onto Kilby Road. There's also a good restaurant and gift shop on the site.

Beyond Harrison Bridge, enjoy the rural quality of the drive into Agassiz. Just before town, Highway 9 leads north to the popular resort village of Harrison Hot Springs, at the south end of Harrison Lake. Here local First Nations, miners and settlers all came to enjoy the healing properties of the natural springs first known as *Kwals* (boiling water) and later as St. Alice's Well. As soon as the CPR arrived, the three-storey, 40-room St. Alice Hotel and Bath House was built; visitors arrived on the railway, then boated upriver to the lake. The first hotel burned down, but it has since been replaced, renovated, updated and expanded and is today decidedly plush.

Lewis Agassiz was the first to settle in the area south of the hot springs, and he called his farm Ferny Coombe. He started the first store and later ran the local post office. The settlement took the name of the farm, but CPR officials thought it just too quaint, and they called their station Agassiz instead—a pity. (Ferny Coombe survives today only as the name of the town swimming pool.) The little town of Agassiz is compact and pretty, centred around the relocated station (now a museum) and with tree-shaded gardens along one side of the main street. Land north of the townsite was set aside in 1888 for the Dominion Experimental Farm, now a federal agricultural research station, so there is plenty of countryside around. Chief crops are hazelnuts and corn, and there is a good local cheese maker. The steep shoulders of Mount Cheam and the Four Brothers in the Skagit Range form an impressive backdrop.

The Coast Mountains come close to the river along its north side, but around Agassiz, there is a fine pocket of agricultural land and many small and pretty farms.

A worthwhile short country drive leads west on Pioneer Avenue following the railway to Ashton Road, then turns south to connect with a pioneer route. Limbert Mountain Road curves through fields and around the steep knob of Cemetery Hill—there's a wonderful leafy heritage cemetery here—to Limbert Mountain Farm, settled in 1902 by the Bouchard family, who planted a vineyard. Still owned by the family, the farm specializes in herbs and heritage produce, and the owners run a small homemade food store and bistro that is popular with food aficionados. The 1912 farmhouse and even some of the original grapevines still survive. Limbert Mountain Road continues west to Cameron Road. A turn north leads across Highway 7 to the Farm House Natural Cheeses shop and farm on McCallum Road.

Back in town, Lougheed Highway (No. 7) proceeds east, then turns abruptly northeast to follow the river alongside the CP rail line. Both road and rail line cut straight across Seabird Island, home of the Seabird Island Band. The island was named after the paddlewheeler *Sea Bird*, which ran aground in the Fraser near here in 1858. The vibrant Sto:lo community lies at the western end of the island alongside Maria Slough, where trumpeter and tundra swans feed and roost in winter. The village is notable for its community school, designed with cedar posts and a soaring shake roof whose angular planes dip and rise like the wings of a bird, and also for its "green" housing complex that uses wind, solar and geothermal power. Seabird Island Road follows the inside edge of the slough and connects with Chaplin and Choate roads to make a short circular driving route. The Seabird Island Band has restored traditional salmon spawning grounds in the shallows near Chaplin Road, and it is also custodian of a small population of the extremely rare Oregon Spotted Frog, now found only in a few locations in the Fraser Valley.

51

Choate Road, which parallels the highway, provides access to farm fields and great mountain views. Various crops are grown here including blueberries, nursery trees and ornamental shrubs—and tulips. In early May, the flower fields are rippling striped carpets of colour against the blue shoulders of Mount Cheam. A tulip festival is held here every spring.

The extension of Highway 7 all the way to Hope was built only in the 1970s. It's a road tightly curtailed by mountain forests on one side and the elevated CP (VIA) railway tracks along the other; the river is seen hardly at all, though there are tantalizing glimpses of the mountains at every turn. The small commercial centre at Ruby Creek, with its excellent First Nations Art Gallery, and the small church of the Sacred Heart on the Chawathil First Nation reserve are a few of the landmarks before the road arrives at Hope.

The First Nation school on Seabird Island is known for its stunning architecture, but heritage is still strong: a tall tribal figure guards the school entrance.

Don't leave Hope without a visit to the Othello-Quintette Tunnels at Othello. Construction of these tunnels was an engineering feat remarkably plotted by Kettle Valley Railway engineer Andrew McCulloch, who, almost a hundred years ago, designed five perfectly aligned tunnels to carry the railway through the sheer granite walls of the twisting Coquihalla River canyon. A walk through the tunnels and across the connecting bridges provides a humbling view of the sheer raw power of the river—and amazement at man's ingenuity. ❖

Halfway between Agassiz and Hope, along the north side of the Fraser, the First Nation community of Chawathil cherishes its small church.

5

PIONEER ROOTS

From B.C.'s capital city, Victoria, the Saanich Peninsula stretches north for 35 kilometres and is bisected by Highway 17, a busy route leading to the airport and the Swartz Bay ferry terminal. This road and the views from its edges are often all that visitors see of this lovely area, but it is possible to avoid the traffic congestion and enjoy the peninsula on smaller, older roads rich with relics of the pioneer era. Here, roadside stands, farm markets, wineries, gardens and berry farms provide more than a taste of country life.

Birders know this area; it's the last place in B.C. where one might find the rare Eurasian skylark, a bird imported from England around the turn of the last century because of its beautiful song: an ascending trill—a love song to its mate—sung only while the bird is rising high into the sky.

Easily covered in a long and lazy day, the route begins and ends in Victoria, whose much-loved cozy quaintness is more than a veneer or a nod to tourism. History really does live here: the streets and alleys reek of it. Originally the home of Salish First Nations, who called the area Camosack (after the wild blue camas they grew for their starchy roots here in carefully tended fields), the city displays a very British heritage dating back to the 1840s, when Vancouver Island was a crown colony. Many buildings in the old part of the city have stories to tell of pioneer life outside the Hudson's Bay Company's Fort Victoria. There are several historic homes here. The 1852 Helmcken House, built by Dr. John Helmcken, is the oldest in B.C. still on its original site; others include the homes of Peter O'Reilly, gold commissioner and judge in the gold-rush days; John Tod, a Hudson's Bay Company trader from Fort Kamloops who retired here; and Emily Carr, the eccentrically brilliant artist and writer. The First Nations presence in the city is strong: there are excellent exhibits in the Royal BC Museum, and Thunderbird Park, beside the museum, has some very fine totems.

Victoria's Dallas Road is a good spot to watch the maritime traffic, particularly at sunset. Here, a pilot boat knifes around from the harbour.

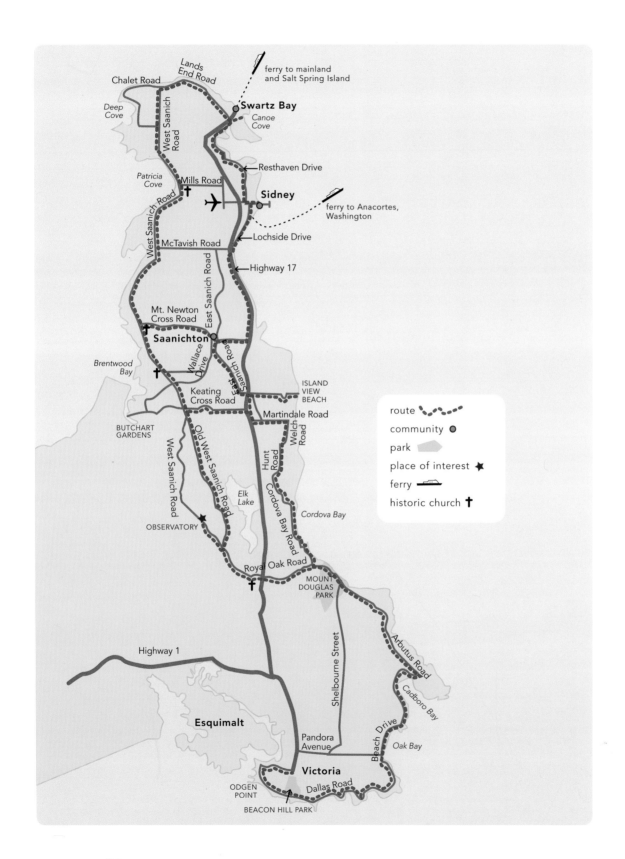

ferry to mainland and Salt Spring Island

Lands End Road

Chalet Road

Swartz Bay

Deep Cove

Canoe Cove

West Saanich Road

Resthaven Drive

Patricia Cove

Mills Road

Sidney

ferry to Anacortes, Washington

West Saanich Road

McTavish Road

Lochside Drive

East Saanich Road

Highway 17

Mt. Newton Cross Road

Saanichton

Wallace Drive

Brentwood Bay

East Saanich Road

ISLAND VIEW BEACH

Keating Cross Road

Martindale Road

BUTCHART GARDENS

Welch Road

West Saanich Road

Old West Saanich Road

Hunt Road

Elk Lake

Cordova Bay Road

Cordova Bay

OBSERVATORY

Royal Oak Road

MOUNT DOUGLAS PARK

Highway 1

Shelbourne Street

Arbutus Road

Cadboro Bay

Esquimalt

Pandora Avenue

Beach Drive

Oak Bay

Victoria

ODGEN POINT

Dallas Road

BEACON HILL PARK

route	
community	⦿
park	▬
place of interest	★
ferry	🛥
historic church	✝

Under a spring canopy of dogwood blossoms, B.C.'s provincial flower, Ross Bay Cemetery houses many pioneer notables.

Victoria is also a very pretty city, its brick buildings and cobbled alleys festooned with hanging baskets and tubs of flowers, and its Inner Harbour promenade anchored by two large and almost ridiculously ornate architectural masterpieces, the Parliament Buildings and the Empress Hotel. From castles to cottages, old inns, churches, schools, emporiums stuffed with British tradition—a day on foot in the city core could not be better spent.

This trip around the Saanich Peninsula starts from Government Street, across the street from the Empress Hotel, and explores first the frilly edges of Victoria's coastline along a road that changes names but is well signposted as the Scenic Marine Drive. Turn right on Belleville Street in front of the Parliament Buildings and follow the route around the edge of the harbour, stopping for a quick look at Fisherman's Wharf, a marina with a colourful mix of boats and floathomes and a good place to buy fresh fish and seafood or hook up with whale-watching tours.

The 32-kilometre scenically sinuous route, at this point called Dallas Road, continues past the Ogden Point Breakwater and Holland Point Park (are there any children sailing their boats on the little pond?) to the south end of Douglas Street. This is Mile Zero, the western start of the Trans-Canada Highway at the edge of Beacon Hill Park. When Victoria was incorporated in 1862, the park area was left outside city limits because of a land dispute, and perhaps that is why the 50-hectare plot of meadows and gardens escaped development. It was made a park in 1882. Even though it is at the heart of the city, the land is wild enough that eagles and blue herons nest here, and in spring the fields sloping down to the shore are still blue with native camas flowers. The Scenic Marine Drive cuts around the edge of the park, always within sight of the walking

*Across the greens
of the Victoria Golf
Club, tiny Trial
Island lighthouse
is backed by the
stupendous backdrop
of Washington's
Olympic Mountains.*

trails along the shore, and continues past Clover Point and on to Ross Bay, where the largest of Victoria's pioneer cemeteries provides a quiet oasis full of ornamental trees and flowers, a fitting last home for many of the early families who helped shape British Columbia's history. Beyond, the road continues a curvy coastline route (King George Terrace) heading toward the Victoria Golf Club—Canada's oldest, founded in 1893 on Gonzales Point at the southwesterly tip of Vancouver Island (this part of the Scenic Marine Drive is called Beach Drive). Across the greens, against the dramatic skyline of the Olympic Mountains, sits the red-roofed lighthouse on tiny Trial Island.

North lies Oak Bay (both the bay and the village were named Oak Bay because of the groves of Garry oaks that once grew here). Oak Bay was once Victoria's seaside resort, reached by city streetcar, and it is known today for its almost exaggerated air of Victorian gentility and English charm, with cozy tea houses and little shops. The Scenic Marine Drive follows Beach Drive, a name it retains through the ritzy area of Uplands and around to Cadboro Bay. The woodlands of Mount Douglas Park, their sinuous arbutus trees and shaggy oaks mingling with evergreens, form a divide from the suburbs of Cordova Bay.

North of the park, turn left on Royal Oak Drive and head inland for a short distance. Cross Highway 17 and then meander north as Royal Oak changes into West Saanich Road and into more bucolic surroundings: preserved farmland here effectively filters the spread of Victoria suburbia. More than 40 small farms and orchards still thrive along the country roads of the peninsula, with its small hills, lovely valleys and whiffs of salt air. The west side, away from the bustle of the highway and its ferry traffic, retains many of its pioneer buildings—beautiful Victorian farmhouses and

cottages, some gilded with architectural gingerbread, and several fine old churches. The first church along the route is St. Michael and All Angels, built in 1883 in Gothic style at the intersection of West Saanich and Wilkinson roads.

A wonderful place to visit, and far quieter than The Butchart Gardens, is Glendale Gardens and Woodland, which has a memorable Japanese garden and a special collection of rhododendrons. From West Saanich Road, turn left on Beaver Lake Road to the garden entrance on Quayle Road.

The neighbourhood of Beaver Lake takes its name from the lake that was connected to larger Elk Lake in 1872 to provide Victoria's main water supply. For years, Elk/Beaver was the freshwater swimming hole of choice for Victorians, who came by horse and buggy and later by railway and trolley for picnics and recreation. In the 1930s, facilities included a tea room, dance hall, boat docks, a roller rink and even, for a while, a chocolate factory.

Oak Bay is known as a very English tweed-and-afternoon-tea community, but it's equally famed for its shoreline view across to Mount Baker.

Today, the lake and its 410 hectares of forest form a regional park. The south entrance is along Beaver Lake Road, where the old store has been turned into a popular restaurant.

Just to the north, the much narrower Old West Saanich Road splits off to the right, but keep straight on West Saanich Road to visit the Dominion Astrophysical Observatory, built in 1916 atop Little Saanich Mountain (also known as Observatory Hill). Still a splendid place to watch the stars (the telescope here was once the world's largest), the observatory and its public interpretive centre (now known as the Centre of the Universe) are worth the steep and winding drive to the rocky summit, not only for the star views, but for the far-reaching island vistas and the spring wildflowers.

Old West Saanich Road, the original pioneer coach road, is the more rural of the two Saanich Roads, and its twists and turns are less travelled. Retrace your steps to the intersection and turn left. A short way north on the old route is

Wild camas grows in profusion in Beacon Hill Park on meadows that were once gardens tended by local First Nations. They grew the blue flowers for their starchy bulbs.

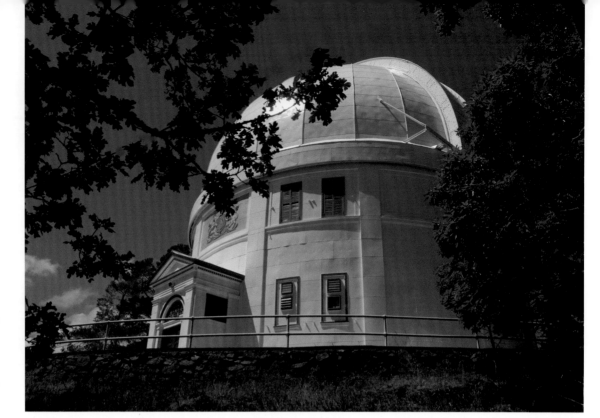

The observatory on Little Saanich Mountain once housed the largest telescope in Canada. Still used for stargazing, the observatory hill also provides great views.

Starling Lane Winery, a small family operation located on farmland acquired in 1859 by Judge Matthew Baillie Begbie, one of B.C.'s most illustrious figures. Begbie brought British law and order to the wild goldfields of the Interior, where he was known, unfairly it seems, as the Hanging Judge. The heritage barn is now the winery store and tasting room. Also on the land is a four-storey water tower and a remarkable white Victorian greenhouse, built recently to an old design.

The older road meanders on, catching up with West Saanich Road again just south of Keating Cross Road. There are several crossroads on the peninsula, and they provide convenient east-west connections. Turning left (west) on Keating leads to Benvenuto Road, past the Victoria Butterfly Gardens and Church & State Wines and on to the floral delights of The Butchart Gardens.

Keep on West Saanich Road through the community of Brentwood Bay—a small ferry here crosses the inlet to Mill Bay, providing a 25-minute shortcut for people heading up-Island (see Chapter 7)— and onto the Tsartlip First Nation reserve. Before Europeans arrived, the Coast Salish people were settled in villages throughout the area, and most of them were persuaded (or tricked) into selling their land to the colony of Vancouver Island so the peninsula could be opened for European settlement. The Douglas Treaties (engineered by James Douglas, then governor of both the Hudson's Bay Company and the Colony) legalized the sale, and land changed ownership in return for a handful of British pounds and a few blankets. From then on, the whole of the Saanich Peninsula belonged to the Crown, except for existing First Nation village sites and fields, which are now reserves. The local Lauwelnew Tribal School, built on the Tsartlip reserve in 1989 to replace a former Catholic institution, is painted with traditional designs, and

The 1860 cemetery beside West Saanich Road is all that is left of a mission that once stood on the Tsartlip reserve. Engulfed in wildflowers, the cemetery includes monuments to several priests who served here.

the entrance has a fascinating bird-sculpture roof. Totems stand above the parking lot. Farther north, across the road, is an 1860 cemetery with simple wooden crosses, marble headstones and a memorial to several priests who served here. Beyond, Our Lady of Assumption Church has been perched on the bluff overlooking Hagen Bight in Saanich Inlet since 1893.

Mount Newton Cross Road, the next east-west connector, is winding and hilly. The fine farmland around it is some of the first in this region to be settled by Europeans, and there are so many pioneer buildings along the four kilometres west to the village of Saanichton that it could easily be called a "heritage road." Right beside the intersection of Mount Newton and West Saanich roads, almost completely hidden by a rampant old-fashioned garden, is Mount Newton Cottage, a pretty little Victorian built in 1893 for Mrs. Betsy Henderson and now operating as a B & B. A short distance east on Mount Newton, a right turn along leafy St. Stephen's Road leads to the oldest church in B.C. still on its original site and in which services have been continuously held since it was built in 1862. St. Stephen's Anglican Church is tiny, built of California redwood, now painted white, with a steep peaked roof and belfry. Guarded by two tall trees, this heritage building is surrounded by a well-tended cemetery that is a beautiful setting, particularly in spring, when clumps of garden primroses and bluebells grow alongside a riotous display of native wildflowers. The church is always open. Don't miss this one: the churchyard gardens, with benches for contemplation, are among the most peaceful anywhere. St. Stephen's is one of several churches in the Victoria area facing closure, but its parishioners and friends have started a trust that aims to keep this lovely heritage church open and in service.

A short distance farther east on Mount Newton's "heritage road" is Bannockburn, a farmhouse almost out of sight below the bank at the foot of Thomson Place, but well marked by a

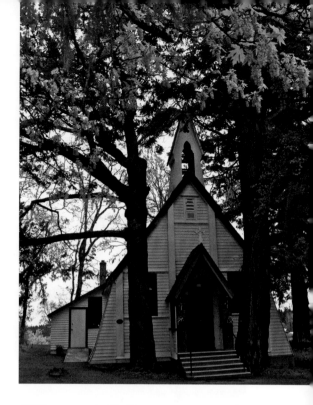

sign. The farmhouse was built by Scottish settler William Thomson, who donated land for St. Stephen's Church and helped with its construction. His story merits telling. As recounted by his great-great-granddaughter, Norma Sealy, he left home at a very early age and came by sailing ship to the west coast, where he was shipwrecked near Clo-oose. He reached the shore and was taken prisoner and held for ransom by local First Nations people. Governor James Douglas bought his freedom for seven wool blankets, and in 1855, Thomson bought this homestead plot, cleared the land for farming and built the house. He married Margaret Lidgate, the daughter of another local settler, and they had 15 children. Bannockburn and its huge farm barn are both heritage buildings. Look for Thomson's grave in St. Stephen's churchyard.

Hidden away in idyllic country surroundings, St. Stephen's church is B.C.'s oldest, in continous service since 1862. Like other small churches with tiny congregations, this historic building faces closure.

Across the road and a little to the west is Butterfield Park and the elegant Edwardian house of Jack Butterfield, captain of the Brentwood Bay/Mill Bay Ferry until 1930. The house dates from 1913 and has heritage status, along with extensive gardens that are currently being restored to their original glory. Planned and nurtured by Butterfield's wife Evelyn and daughter Hilda, the gardens were once elegant and colourful with massed displays of flowers including 40 varieties of iris, a rose garden and flowering shrubs. The estate featured an orchard, vegetable garden, and even an outdoor aviary and a tennis court. The house is open to the public only one day a year, but the grounds have become a park; the garden paths among the flower beds invite dalliance. Other heritage sites along Mount Newton Cross Road include the 1853 Lidgate homestead, Rose Farm (1890), which has a stone creamery and 1907 barn, and the 1900 Nickels farmhouse. But this road offers more than a heritage tour: it is also one of the most prettily rural stretches in the area, with views of rolling pastureland, sheep, cows, farm markets and vineyards.

Rising north of the road, Mount Newton is a site of spiritual importance to Vancouver Island First Nations. In their oral history, this peak and Mount Malahat across Saanich Inlet were the only lands to escape their great creation flood. Mount Newton and its forests, including some of the last stands of mature Douglas fir and Garry oak on the peninsula, are now preserved in John Dean Provincial Park.

Our Lady of Assumption, seen here framed by purple thistles, is another of the pioneer churches along the west side of the Saanich Peninsula. It dates from 1893.

From Mount Newton Cross Road, West Saanich Road winds north, a bit too far from the inlet to see very much of it through the trees and shrubs until it reaches Coles Bay. At the south end, where the road meets tidewater, the Pauquachin First Nation reserve is home to another of the tribes involved in the Douglas Treaties. But in an interesting reversal of history, this tribe may regain some of the lands it lost. It has negotiated sole rights to buy back a large area of forest along with Dunsmuir Lodge, the now-closed 45-room hotel and conference centre owned by the University of Victoria.

North of Coles Bay, West Saanich Road curves around to Patricia Bay, where much of the land to the east is occupied by the Victoria International Airport. Along the shore, a large conglomeration of federal buildings houses the Institute of Ocean Sciences, the headquarters of the Canadian Coast Guard Pacific Fleet, and the Pacific Geoscience Centre, the main B.C. earthquake monitoring station, which sits, appropriately enough, on one of the west coast's seismic faults. These facilities are not generally open to the public. Birders might want to prowl along the airport fence; this is one of the areas where the few remaining skylarks breed and sing. Birding is good here, too, for winter shorebirds. West Saanich Road here runs very close to the shore, providing beach access and good views of maritime activities.

Just past the airport, Mills Road cuts east, and on the corner sits another small heritage church, Holy Trinity, built in 1895 and surrounded by another flowery graveyard, this one shaded with oak and yew trees planted in 1937 to commemorate the coronation of King George VI. A warning sign in front reads "Thou Shalt Not Park," so pull off into the approved lot around the

OPPOSITE *Two gulls sail the apricot seas at the Sidney waterfront, which looks east across the Gulf Islands and enjoys flamboyant sunrises.*

corner for a walk through the old churchyard, and to scan the heavens for skylarks. Their angelic song, once heard, will never be forgotten.

West Saanich Road goes straight north from Patricia Bay past tiny Tseycum First Nation reserve and into Deep Cove. Detour via Birch and Chalet roads to visit Muse Winery and Deep Cove Chalet, which boast extensive beachside gardens and a reputation for haute cuisine. Built in 1914, the attractive old premises were at the terminus of the former B.C. Electric Railway inter-urban line from Victoria. (It is interesting to reflect that tiny Saanich Peninsula was once served by three railways, all now defunct and mostly converted to hiking trails.) At the northern tip of Deep Cove is Moses Point, which has a small park and beach. Here Chalet Road becomes Lands End Road and runs along the forested northern edge of the peninsula heading for the Swartz Bay ferry. It overpasses the highway and leads to Canoe Cove marina, crammed with small boats and housing the Victoria area's only heritage pub, the Stonehouse, built in the 1930s.

Canoe Cove is almost isolated by Highway 17. To escape south, travellers must join the highway traffic for a short distance, then exit almost at once onto McDonald Park Road. This leads south along the shore of Blue Heron Basin and from here, Resthaven Drive curves around into the town of Sidney (or Sidney-by-the-Sea). Sidney harbour walkway and wharf provide outstanding views to the mainland, where the snow cone of Mount Baker floats above a maze of islands. A large sawmill that once occupied the site here was the impetus for the 1894 construction of the Victoria and Sidney Railway, whose major freight was cordwood to fuel the furnaces and fireplaces of downtown Victoria. Known affectionately as the "Cordwood Limited," it ran until 1919. From the Sidney wharf, steamships once provided service to the Lower Mainland via Port Guichon, near Ladner. Sidney today retains a distinct village character, with small interesting shops along Beacon Street and a very popular farmers' market. It is home to so many independent bookstores that it has earned a reputation as the "Book Capital of B.C."

From the wharf, take First Street and drive south along the shore past the terminal for Washington State's ferries to Anacortes and join Lochside Drive, which is on the roadbed of another railway, the Canadian National, which runs parallel to Highway 17 around the shore of Bazan Bay. At the northern edge of the Tsawout First Nation reserve, the railway right-of-way reverts to a hiking/biking trail known as Lochside Regional Trail, and Lochside Drive comes to an end. Our route crosses the highway at the traffic lights onto Mount Newton Cross Road and heads into the central hub village of Saanichton. Here, where three old roads—East Saanich, Wallace and Mount Newton—converge, is the balconied Prairie Inn. Surrounded in spring by red rhododendrons, this historic hostelry built by former HBC baker Henry Simpson has been serving travellers on the coach road from Victoria since 1858. The present building, which closely follows the form of the first, dates from 1893. Saanichton is home to western Canada's oldest agricultural fair, founded in

A great blue heron flies leisurely over Island View Beach at morning low tide. Well named, the beach is a prime birdwatching spot.

1871. In spring, the fields of several of the farms around the village turn gold with daffodils.

Leave Saanichton on East Saanich Road and continue south to Island View Road, following it across Highway 17. To the north beside the Lochside Regional Trail are the extensive grounds of the Saanich Historical Artifacts Society, a volunteer organization dedicated to the preservation and restoration of old farm equipment and steam engines—lots of them. Nearby is one of Victoria's favourite farm stores, Michell Bros. Farm, in a big barn well stocked with homegrown fruits and vegetables. Island View Road continues east to a park along the shore known as Island View Beach. Piled with driftwood and with trails through the salt marshes, this waterfront park provides a great rest stop before the journey home and is an excellent place for birdwatching at low tide.

To reach another good birding spot, perhaps the very best on the peninsula, return to Highway 17 and drive south for about one kilometre, then turn left (east) onto Martindale Road. This leads through marshy flatland fields (Martindale Flats) known to be favoured by skylarks and many other birds, particularly during spring and fall migrations. In April, daffodils cover the slopes above the unnamed creek.

This country road ends here, for Victoria is very close, and Highway 17 is a fast return route to downtown. But if you choose to stay off the highway and to wander around Martindale Flats with your binoculars, go south on Welch Road, which turns into Hunt Road, then south again on Fowler Road to Cordova Bay Road. Here you can return to the highway or retrace your steps along the Scenic Marine Drive back to Victoria's Inner Harbour, where you started out. ❖

6

COAST ROAD TO RENFREW

Vancouver Island's west coast is rocky and wild, facing the onslaught of fierce storms that pick up maximum speed as they hurl in across the Pacific Ocean, bringing lashings of rain and high winds. Where the land meets the sea, it is frayed into islands, carved into rocky promontories, scooped out into sandy bays and shredded into long meandering inlets. Often shrouded with fog, the coast is—or was, for a very long time—impenetrable, a dense thicket of forest covering the bony knees and elbows of some of the fiercest mountains on earth—young mountains, hung with glaciers and topped by granite crags not yet smoothed into any resemblance of softness.

It is known as a graveyard for ships, hundreds of them. Canoes and sailing ships, steel-hulled cargo vessels, passenger liners, fishboats, tugboats—all have come to grief on the rocks, and the few survivors who made it to shore usually perished in the hostile wilderness. As maritime traffic along the coast increased, so did the number of wrecks. The situation reached a crisis in 1906 when the *Valencia* came to grief at Pachena Point where, in full sight of land, 126 lives were lost. To bring help to future stranded mariners, a telegraph line was strung between trees along the most wreck-prone section of the coast, 80 kilometres north from Port Renfrew to Bamfield, and a rough trail was hacked out alongside the line. Huts provided shelter for the telegraph linesmen and for shipwreck survivors. This life-saving trail was kept in operation for many years, eventually falling into disrepair as more efficient means of weather forecasting and navigation reduced ship casualties. It has since been restored and is now the West Coast Trail, one of the most famous—and most gruelling—wilderness hiking trails in the world.

There are only a few continuous stretches of road along this rugged west coast. The best known, from Ucluelet to Tofino, a section famous for its beautiful sand beaches, is reached by highway from Port Alberni. The longest (although it runs north a mere 100 kilometres from

Sooke's public wharf is on the protected waters of Sooke Bay, home to a large fishing fleet. East Sooke Park lies along the far shore.

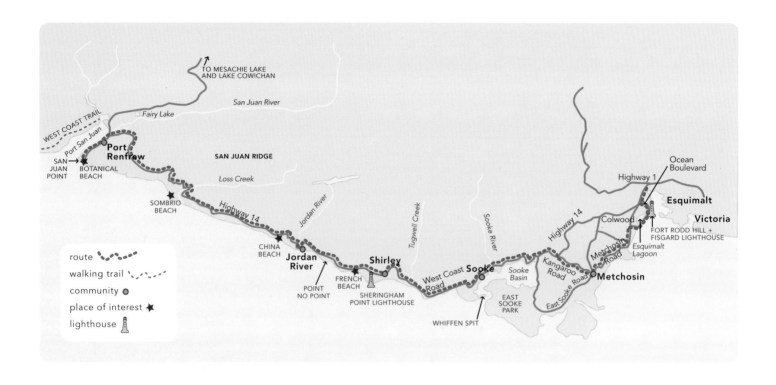

Esquimalt to Port Renfrew) is known from Sooke onward as the West Coast Road (or Highway 14). Within easy reach of urban Victoria, it is narrow, curvy and leads to some of the oldest settlements and prettiest beaches and shorelines on the Island. For day trippers, Port Renfrew is the turnaround point. (But it could also be the start of wilder adventures, since the southern end of the West Coast Trail starts here.)

Begin this excursion to the West Coast Road by leaving Victoria on the Trans-Canada Highway (Highway 1) and heading north across the mouth of Portage Inlet. Exit onto the Island Highway, the pioneer coach road from Victoria to Sooke. At the north end of Parson's Bridge is the Six Mile Pub, established here in 1855 by Bill Parson and enjoying almost continuous operation ever since. The Six Mile became a roadhouse in the 1880s when stagecoaches stopped here to deliver mail and passengers. The present creekside premises date from the early 1900s. Across the bridge (which spans Millstream Creek, a source of fresh water for early ships), at the top end of Esquimalt Harbour, the road enters the suburban strip of Colwood. Turn left at the traffic lights onto Ocean Boulevard and follow it to Fort Rodd Hill, an artillery fort built in 1895 to guard the naval base at Esquimalt across the inlet. A National Historic Site, the fort's grounds are manicured lawns (perfect for picnicking), the old brick residences, barracks and gun emplacements on the high bluffs have been stabilized and interpreted, and, in summer months, the old canteen building sells refreshments.

On a tiny island at the very tip of the point is Fisgard Lighthouse, the first to be built on Canada's west coast. The tall, whitewashed tower and the two-storey keeper's house were built in 1860 from bricks brought around Cape Horn as ballast in sailing ships. Connected to the mainland by a rock causeway, the lighthouse is also a National Historic Site, and is well interpreted for visitors. The keeper's house is now a museum. Allow at least an hour to enjoy it all.

Ocean Boulevard continues southwest to cross a narrow humpbacked bridge onto the Coburg Peninsula, a long, narrow strand dividing the ocean from Esquimalt Lagoon. This is one stretch where extra-slow driving is called for, not because it is dangerous, but because it is so beautiful. On one side of the road, a pebble beach piled with driftwood and washed by ocean waves looks across to the

The oldest on the B.C. coast, the 1860 Fisgard Lighthouse—now a museum—was built with stone brought over as ballast in sailing ships. Along with adjacent Fort Rodd Hill, it is now a National Historic Site.

Olympic mountains of Washington; on the other side, across from Royal Roads University (once a military college), the quiet lagoon is always full of ducks, geese, swans and other birds. The salt lagoon and the beach foreshore are protected within a federal Migratory Bird Sanctuary: the area is well known for huge flocks of brant geese that overwinter in the eelgrass here.

Continue along the peninsula almost to its end, then head up Lagoon Road to Metchosin Road and turn left (west) toward the village of Metchosin. Along the way is Witty's Lagoon park, another prime birders' destination. The first entrance to Witty's is a trail leading from the parking lot down through ferny woods and a salt marsh to the beach. The trail passes Sitting Lady Falls, a 30-metre double plunge whose formation evokes the very appropriate name. Look for ladyslipper orchids here in spring.

Metchosin's old village is centred around the church and store at the intersection with Happy Valley Road. Built in 1873, the pretty little church of St. Mary the Virgin is better known to some as St. Mary of the Lilies. In April, the surrounding graveyard, shaded by Garry oaks, is

LEFT *The graveyard around St. Mary's Church in Metchosin is kept wild because of the flowers that bloom here: erythroniums (or lilies) in the spring, white daisies in the summer.*

snowy with the nodding heads of white erythroniums, known locally as Easter lilies. White daisies take their place in summer. The grass between the graves is left uncut to allow the wild-flowers to go to seed. It's a peaceful spot at any time of year, and its ethereal beauty gives cause to linger.

Take Happy Valley Road right past the 1872 pioneer schoolhouse/museum, then turn left on Rocky Point Road and right again onto Kangaroo Road. At the intersection is an access point for a regional park, one that is only 30 metres wide but 47 kilometres long. This is the abandoned roadbed of the CN Railway, now a trail known as the Galloping Goose, named for the noisy gas-driven railcar that carried passengers between Victoria and Sooke in the 1920s. The rail line once ran all the way around Sooke Basin and up to copper and gold mines along the Sooke River. Canada's first rails-to-trails conversion, the Galloping Goose is a popular hiking, biking and horseback route.

Kangaroo Road, long, winding and wooded, connects with Highway 14 (Sooke Road), which leads to Sooke and beyond. Turning west, the highway passes the Tudor-style 17 Mile House Pub, another of the old coaching inns whose name marked the distance from Victoria. Built in 1893, it has been serving good cheer ever since, and is reputed to be haunted. The highway continues down to the scalloped north shore of Sooke Basin, a large body of protected water accessible from Juan de Fuca Strait through a very narrow neck that is almost closed off by the sandy hook of Whiffen Spit. The Sooke River flows into the basin just before the town of Sooke. Discovery of gold upstream caused a local but ephemeral stampede: a gold camp called

OPPOSITE *In Witty's Lagoon park, trails lead down to the beach past the aptly named Sitting Lady Falls.*

72

Leechtown was hastily thrown up and equally hastily abandoned. Nothing of Leechtown now remains, except for a commemorative marker. More accessible upriver is Sooke Potholes park, where the water has worn huge basins into the glaciated bedrock—perfect pools for summer dips. Turn right up Sooke River Road just before the bridge. The area here is still known as Milnes Landing, named after settler Edward Milne, who opened a store here in 1893 and built a wharf so he could bring supplies in by boat; there's a store here still.

Across the bridge is the excellent Sooke Region Museum and Visitor Centre, strikingly identified at the roadside by the red and white original light (technically a first-order Fresnel lens) taken from the Triangle Island lighthouse at the extreme northern tip of Vancouver Island. Moss Cottage, a sweet diminutive house built in 1870 for James and Mary Ellen Walsh and their six children, was moved next to the museum. (The oldest pioneer home in Sooke, it was called Moss Cottage not because of the moss on the roof but for Mary's mother's maiden name.)

Sooke has a long history. Manuel Quimper claimed the bay for Spain in 1791, naming it Puerta de Revilla Gigedo. Six years later, when the Spanish withdrew their claim to the coast, the area was re-surveyed by the British, who gave British names to everything in sight except for Sooke itself, which already had a well-established local name, T'Sou-ke, the name of the First Nation that resides here still. At Maple Avenue, which leads down to the Government Wharf, a cairn commemorates the landing of the first European settler, William Grant, who arrived with eight workers from Scotland in 1849 to build a sawmill and homestead here. He stayed only a brief time, but he left a colourful and perhaps unfortunate legacy. On his Sooke property he planted seeds of English broom, a hardy little shrub that flourished and spread like wildfire, adding torches of bright gold all over southern Vancouver Island. Above the harbour, Broom Hill commemorates Grant's gift, now considered a noxious weed, and higher up, Mount Manuel Quimper surveys all the land that its namesake once claimed for Spain. North on Maple Avenue is the pioneer cemetery in Centennial Park.

Grant may have been the first settler, but the Muir family is considered Sooke's first permanent white residents. They, too, left a legacy: a couple of outstanding heritage homes. The 1870 two-storey Georgian farmhouse, Woodside, beside the highway just west of the village centre, was the home of John and Ann Muir, who came to B.C. from Scotland with their daughter and four sons to manage the Hudson's Bay Company coal mines at Fort Rupert in 1849. Later they moved to Fort Victoria before claiming Crown land at Sooke. Here, they started in the logging business, built a steam-operated sawmill and a boat-building enterprise. One of the sons, Michael, and his wife Matilda later commissioned an equally gracious abode, Burnside Farm, on Maple Avenue. Both these heritage homes are still in impeccable condition and both are in private hands. Burnside is a B & B.

The heritage church of the Holy Trinity on Murray Street did not survive a disastrous fire; however, its modern replacement is worth seeing for its perennial gardens, ablaze with summer

Old wharf pilings stretch into Sooke Basin, a large natural harbour almost closed off at its mouth by Whiffen Spit.

colour. At the foot of Murray, a path leads onto a boardwalk trail to the Rotary Pier for good views of the Sooke waterfront. The Government Wharf is the place to go to enjoy the salty ambience of a fishing port, though only a few of the really old buildings are still standing. Ask about sightseeing and whale-watching trips, or kayak rentals. Sooke Road officially becomes West Coast Road at the Government Wharf.

One vantage point not to be missed on the western edge of the town is Whiffen Spit, the long curving sandspit that almost blocks the entrance to Sooke Harbour. The road is very well signposted, for on the Spit sits Sooke Harbour House, one of the best eating establishments anywhere, known for its culinary inventiveness and use of fresh, mostly homegrown produce. A sturdy walking trail extending the length of Whiffen Spit is popular with hikers, dog walkers and birders. With waves dashing on the ocean side, and calm water on the inside, the Spit is a good walk at any time of year.

Beyond Whiffen Spit, the winding West Coast Road continues along the shore, although seaward views are mostly obscured by thick second-growth forest. Watch for llamas at the intersection of Otter Point Road (a rambling high road that leads back into Sooke), and farther along, the sign to Tugwell Creek Honey Farm Meadery, whose honey-based wines are made (in part) by the thousands of bees buzzing around the 100 hives in the wildflower meadows. The first meadery in B.C., Tugwell makes prizewinning ancient brews with such lovely names as Solstice Metheglin, Melomel, and Wassail Gold. Beekeeping courses are also offered here.

The first open stretch of shoreline along the West Coast Road is at Gordon Beach, where a fine pebble beach thick with driftwood provides great views across the strait to the Olympic

The road to Port Renfrew cuts through forest still inhabited by wildlife, including bears. Here, twin cubs play balance on the road barrier; the mother bear scuttled out of sight.

Mountains. The road heads inland again through forest to the hamlet of Shirley. Founded in 1885, it is marked today by its large community hall. Turn left here along Sheringham Point Road and drive out through a newly surveyed housing development onto the cliffs. The 1912 lighthouse, now fully automated, is closed to the public, but informal trails lead from the gate left along the wire fence and out onto the headland for a quintessential lighthouse view: an elegant white tower on top of rugged cliffs, with waves swirling at its feet.

From here almost all the way to Port Renfrew, the road is hemmed in by forest on both sides, and the string of fine beaches along the shore is mostly out of sight. However, one can drive right in to French Beach, a popular provincial park and a good place for beachcombing. Farther along, the tea house and cabins that opened at Point No Point in 1952 have been upgraded into an elegant resort and restaurant, though some of the cabins have preserved their rustic ambience. The great sunsets remain unrivalled. It's one of the few places along the coast here where the road comes close enough to the cliff edge to afford a spectacular view. Sandcut Beach, a few kilometres farther north, is reached by a 10-minute hike along a steep forest trail, a trek well worth the effort. A creek tumbles from overhanging sandstone cliffs in two cascades down onto the beach. Look for the trail sign along the road.

Jordan River was named not for the biblical River Jordan but for the chaplain of Francisco de Eliza, the Spanish explorer who sailed south along the coast from Nootka in 1791. At the mouth of Jordan River, the former logging community fronts a wide bay lined with a broad shingle beach. The waves race in here, creating wonderful rollers for surfing. Just before the big log bridge, a small campsite and picnic area on the spit provide excellent viewing of the surfing acrobatics and, in winter, of black-legged kittiwakes in the tide rips at the river mouth. From the beach, the unobstructed view across to the Olympic Peninsula, stretching from Cape Flattery to Port Angeles, can be inspirational, particularly at sunset. There's a store and eateries here, but no gas station.

The Jordan River hydroelectric plant was finished in 1911 and still provides hydro power for most of southern Vancouver Island. During its construction a hundred years ago, a thousand workers were shipped in by boat to what used to be an isolated coastal settlement—there was then no road any farther west than Sooke. A 40-metre-high diversion dam built upstream was once the highest in Canada, and a long wooden flume led the water down to a power plant at the river mouth. The system operated, with a few improvements, until 1971, when the flume was replaced by a tunnel leading to a new power plant located upstream. A few remains of the original power plant can be found in the roadside undergrowth.

The West Coast Road (extended north from Jordan River only in 1975 and paved in 1980) was built inland from the craggy coast and runs through forests now well into their second- and third-growth cycle since the virgin timber was cut. China Beach, which has vehicle access and campsites, anchors the south end of the 55-kilometre-long Juan de Fuca Marine Trail, a wilderness coastal path that travels through provincial parkland all the way to the tip of San Juan Point near Port Renfrew. Unlike its more popular counterpart, the West Coast Trail, which demands a heavy commitment of time and energy, the Juan de Fuca Trail stays relatively close to the highway all the way, with four well-signed access points en route, allowing for smaller gulps of coastal wilderness—even day hikes. The trail, though rugged, is well maintained, and there are several high suspension bridges to cross, one within easy reach of the China Beach day use area.

Motorists driving along the West Coast Road—which, after Jordan River, climbs increasingly higher onto the forested slopes of San Juan Ridge—might be completely unaware of the shoreline beauty that lies far below them. At Loss Creek, the road switchbacks sharply upstream to cross the creek on an old log bridge. Here, a small park protects a virgin grove of tall Sitka spruce. Farther along, an easy trail leads down to Sombrio Beach, a place where surfers hang out, waiting for the waves, at about the halfway point along the Juan de Fuca Trail. There's a small cave and waterfall here, where local First Nations once came to bathe, believing Sombrio to be the warmest place on the island. The trail continues all the way to Port Renfrew.

As the West Coast Road nears its end, it veers away from the coast, then makes an abrupt turn and swings around the south shore of Port San Juan (Puerto de San Juan), before diving into the town of Port Renfrew. Manuel Quimper, who named the natural harbour, anchored his ships at the river mouth and sent a mule train expedition to the headwaters of the river in a fruitless search for gold. When, almost a century later, Hugh McKay of Sooke came to investigate

From China Beach to Port Renfrew, the Juan de Fuca Marine Trail cuts along the wild and rocky shoreline. The 55-kilometre-long hiking trail can be accessed at several points along the road.

the Spanish diggings, he found two other hopeful miners already at work. Only traces of gold rewarded their efforts.

The first European settlement at the river mouth was known as San Juan until homesteaders found their mail was commonly being directed to San Juan in the U.S. Gulf Islands. The name was then changed to Port Renfrew to honour Lord Renfrew, whose promised scheme to settle Scottish crofters here never materialized. Port Renfrew is the start (or end) of both the arduous West Coast Trail along the wreck-strewn coast to Bamfield, 80 tough kilometres north, and the Juan de Fuca Trail. The town has long been dependent on forestry and fishing, but recently it has expanded its commercial prospects to include tourism. With the two popular long-distance hiking trails, a growing interest in wildlife watching and a recently paved cross-Island route through the forest to Cowichan Lake, Port Renfrew could very well become one of Vancouver Island's premier destinations. At present though, despite an influx of international clientele, the village is still decidedly rustic—and that is its charm.

The West Coast Road rides straight into town, coming to a halt at the historic Port Renfrew Hotel at the Government Wharf. This country road ends here, although there are still many more places to explore: Snuggery Cove beside the wharf is most photogenic, with lots of boats and fresh fish and prawns for sale. Cross the long bridge at the head of Port San Juan (the mouth of the estuary still keeps its older name), where wood cut from huge spruce trees was once shipped out for early airplane construction. Follow logging roads to Fairy and Lizard lakes, or continue on the paved road to Cowichan Lake. There are several Big Trees to visit: the Red Creek Fir, the

Harris Creek Spruce and Grant's Grove of giant firs and cedars.

However, Botanical Beach, if the tide is low, could be the highlight of your trip. A spectacular area of intertidal strand, the shoreline here contains rock pools hollowed out by the ocean and exposed at low tide, trapping creatures of the sea normally seen only by divers. Reached by road from Port Renfrew (turn left just before the Government Wharf) and within a 15-minute walk of a parking lot, the low-tide aquaria contain such colourful creatures as starfish, sea anemones and urchins, small fish and crabs, and wonderful gardens of undersea weeds. Home to the world's first marine research station (the University of Minnesota set up camp here in 1900) and a gun emplacement during the Second World War, the beach today and its wave-worn cliffs are a wilderness treasure. It's a wonderful place to end the day. ✤

At low tide, the rocky shore at Botanical Beach, pitted with fissures and tide pools, provides a marine biology lesson. The pools trap sea anemones, starfish and other underwater denizens. The beach is easily reached from Port Renfrew.

7

COWICHAN COASTAL ROAD

The Trans-Canada Highway leads north from Victoria to Nanaimo, cutting, for the most part, inland from the coastal plain. But the older country roads—slower, and far more interesting—wander around the Island's east coast bays and inlets, linking the farms and villages that give it its pastoral charm. On this entrancing route from Mill Bay to Ladysmith, there are enough farm gate offerings to more than fill a picnic basket—everything from fresh eggs, fruits, cheese, crusty breads, wine and cider. And, for a visual feast, how about fields of lavender?

Begin this country drive from Victoria the easy way by taking "Vancouver's Island's most beautiful shortcut": the ferry from Brentwood Bay to Mill Bay, a 25-minute ride across Saanich Inlet. This oldest government ferry service on the B.C. coast started in the 1920s with a converted wooden tramp steamer. After years of mishaps and refits, the ship was replaced in 1956 by the specially commissioned steel-hulled *Mill Bay*, which has made the crossing 18 times a day ever since. It is indeed a scenic ride, with extensive views (from the open car deck) north up the Inlet and across to the towering hump of Mount Malahat, a mountain still held sacred by the Malahat First Nation. The scar on the forested hillside is the abandoned B.C. Cement Company factory site and wharf at Bamberton. Bamberton Provincial Park, with a sandy beach and campsites, is adjacent.

Across the Inlet, turn right (north) from the ferry landing and follow Mill Bay Road along the beaches and tree-lined shore (no suburban streets, it's reserve land, kept much the way it has always looked), past the Government Wharf to the commuter town of Mill Bay, so called because of the sawmills that once flourished here. The road goes through town to join Highway 1 (the Trans-Canada). Drive north on the highway a short distance to Shawnigan Lake Road and go left toward the village of the same name, turning onto Cameron Taggart Road to visit Merridale

Damali Lavender Farm near Cowichan Bay has branched out: it is also a winery and a very lovely B & B.

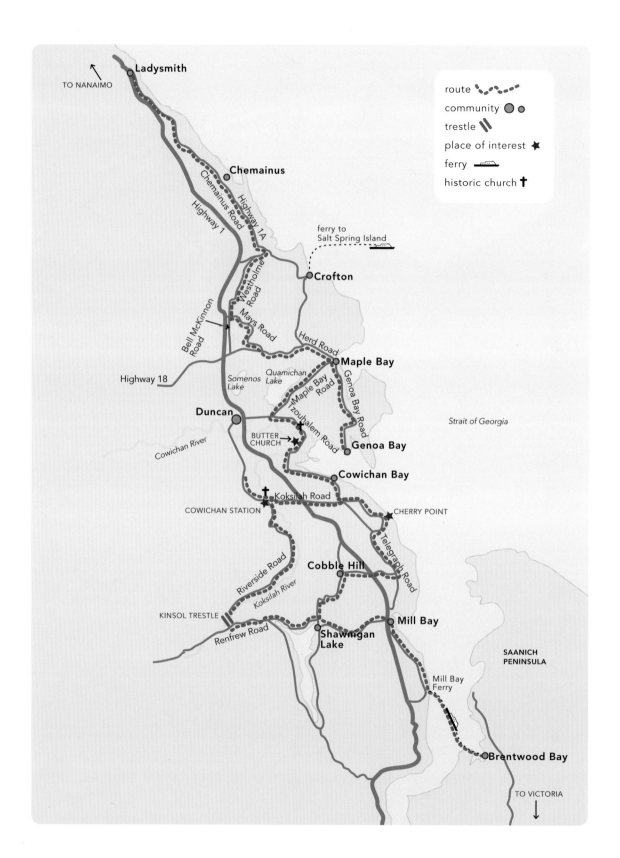

route ⌇

community ● ●

trestle ⫽

place of interest ★

ferry 🚢

historic church ✝

Ladysmith

TO NANAIMO

Chemainus

Chemainus Road

Highway 1A

Highway 1

ferry to
Salt Spring Island

Westholme Road

Crofton

Bell McKinnon Road

Mays Road

Herd Road

Highway 18

Somenos Lake

Quamichan Lake

Maple Bay

Maple Bay Road

Genoa Bay Road

Duncan

Cowichan River

BUTTER CHURCH

Tzouhalem Road

Strait of Georgia

Genoa Bay

Cowichan Bay

Koksilah Road

COWICHAN STATION

CHERRY POINT

Telegraph Road

Cobble Hill

Riverside Road

Koksilah River

KINSOL TRESTLE

Renfrew Road

Shawnigan Lake

Mill Bay

SAANICH
PENINSULA

Mill Bay
Ferry

Brentwood Bay

TO VICTORIA

While trains no longer travel over it, the high wooden Kinsol Trestle, west of Shawnigan Lake, now forms part of the Trans-Canada Trail.

Ciderworks. The largest cider orchard in Canada, it grows heritage apples with such lovely old names as Tremlett's Bitter and Yarlington Mill. In summer, the place is awash with blossoms and buzzing with bees. The Ciderworks and its popular bistro have everything to please the traveller including guided tours, tastings, a farm store and a wonderful country ambience.

The village of Shawnigan Lake (beside the lake of the same name) began in 1881 with three sawmills, all eventually destroyed by fire. When the Esquimalt and Nanaimo Railway came through in 1886 (the E & N was built by coal baron Robert Dunsmuir in return for the 20 percent of Vancouver Island that contained all the known coal reserves), the sawmill settlement became a popular resort area. There were two fine hotels, the Strathcona and the Shawnigan Lake, and weekend trippers arrived in droves to picnic, fish and swim. Today, it's more of a commuter community, with upscale new shops beside the old-time Aitken & Fraser General Store. The church has been converted to a restaurant.

At the northeast corner of the lake, Shawnigan Lake/Mill Bay Road meets Renfrew Road, an inland logging road to Port Renfrew that starts here but is now closed because of an unsafe suspension bridge. Drive along Renfrew Road to see the incredible Kinsol Trestle, a wooden span high above the Koksilah River that once carried the CN railway and now hosts the right-of-way for the Cowichan Valley Trail (part of the Trans-Canada Trail network). The Kinsol Trestle is 187 metres long by 44 metres high, the highest and longest in Canada and one of the four largest in the world. For several years, rotting timbers and arson damage closed the 1920 heritage structure, last crossed by train in 1979, but it is undergoing renovation and is scheduled to open in

2011 for hikers and cyclists. A walk across its spidery heights is a thrill. Access its south end from Renfrew Road via Glen Eagles and Shelby Road. The trestle's north end can be reached by driving 8.5 kilometres south down Riverside Road from its junction with Koksilah Road, near Cowichan Station.

Return to the Shawnigan Lake village centre and then drive north along Shawnigan Lake Road to Cobble Hill, a very early farm settlement—it has hosted an agricultural fair every year since 1909—that maintains the feel of an English village, though it has shrunk from its former two-hotel status. The E & N Railway still stops here: look for the tiny station on the main street. From the village centre, take Hutchinson Road east and cross Highway 1 to Telegraph Road, where sloping fields of lavender spread a summer haze of purple. Damali Lavender Farm, which is also a winery and a B & B, has a well-stocked gift shop. Telegraph Road continues

The Esquimalt and Nanaimo Railway still chugs along the coast twice a day, stopping at several places, including the diminutive Cowichan Station, its tiny waiting room hung with flowers.

north through farmland to Cherry Point Road. Turn right here, particularly if you wish to visit the popular winery. A further right turn onto Garnet Road leads to Cherry Point Nature Observation Park, which has a good beach and tidal flats. Cherry Point Road rambles and angles and, at a 90-degree bend, merges into Koksilah Road. Cowichan Bay Road, the suggested route, leads north a short distance beyond.

But first, Koksilah Road itself makes an interesting side trip. Follow it west across Highway 1 and under the E & N Railway Bridge. Turn right here to see St. Andrew's Church (1906), painted a soft red; turn left to see tiny Cowichan Station, hung with baskets of pink petunias. Koksilah Road crosses a narrow bridge across the Koksilah River. (Riverside Road, on the left, leads to the Kinsol Trestle, described earlier.) A right turn on Tigwell Road one kilometre farther leads to Bright Angel Park, where woodland trails on both sides of the river are connected by a high suspension bridge. The park is popular for picnics, and the river forms deep swimming holes among the rocks. Continue on Koksilah Road another four kilometres to Miller Road and turn left almost immediately into the driveway leading to Keating Farm Estate, now in the hands of The Land Conservancy of B.C. Dating from the 1880s, it's still a working farm with an orchard, hayfields, bees and chickens, several barns and outbuildings—but it's the farmhouse that draws the most attention. The original house was small, but in 1894, architect John Tiarks designed a huge new addition, which included a two-storey "great hall" with a vaulted ceiling. Constructed of first-growth cedar and fir, the addition turned the modest farmhouse into a mansion. On summer Sunday afternoons, the heritage farm (including the house) is open for tours.

Return on Koksilah Road to Cowichan Bay Road and follow it north around the shore to the community of Cowichan Bay, where a colourful assortment of pioneer buildings crowds the road and juts out over the beach. There is a pleasantly ramshackle air to this workaday but very popular spot, with its gaggle of small food shops, galleries, markets, and cafes cheek by jowl with marine supply stores, boat builders and tour operators providing whale-watching and kayak tours. The Columbia Hotel, built here in the 1860s, is now the Masthead Restaurant. Stop for a stroll along the Government Wharf or visit the Cowichan Wooden Boat Society and Cowichan Bay Maritime Centre at the end of the dock. Hecate Park just north of the village is a good place to leave the car while you explore.

The road continues around Cowichan Bay within easy view of the mud flats. Two rivers, the Koksilah and the Cowichan, enter the bay almost side by side, and the estuary is a maze of channels and tributaries. At a wide spot on the left side of the road overhung with trees, a modest stone cairn and plaque commemorate the 1862 landing of the first group of farm settlers, brought here on the HMS *Hecate* by the Hudson's Bay Company. The Cowichan Valley has been a farmer's stronghold ever since.

Another sign on a stone seat tells the world that Yukon poet Robert Service lived here in the 1890s. Working as a writer in the evenings, he had various day jobs, at a local dairy farm and as a clerk in the Corfield family store, which used to be near the bridge here. Less than a kilometre beyond, Cowichan Bay Road takes a sharp left around the grounds of the South Cowichan Lawn Tennis Club, whose grass courts, established in the Victorian era around 1887 and still very much in use, are second only to Wimbledon's in terms of antiquity. On the shore side, Maple Grove Park was named for the giant bigleaf maples on the site. The estuary is a prime waterfowl area, known for trumpeter swans and great blue herons. More than 200 different species of birds have been seen here, and bald eagles frequent the beaches and treetops. There is a Nature Trust bird blind along Lochmanetz Road.

At the tennis courts corner, keep straight onto Tzouhalem Road,

Cowichan Bay village clings to the shore, fringed with wharves and marinas. Shops and restaurants, whale-watching tours and kayak trips make this place very popular.

which cuts across the mouth of the estuary, bridging the various arms of the rivers. Much of the land near here is part of the Cowichan Tribes reserve. On the left side of the road on top of a rocky knoll known as Comiaken Hill sits a large, well made and beautifully proportioned stone church built in 1870 by Father Peter Rondeault. The Oblate missionary arrived in Victoria and was paddled by canoe to the First Nation village of Clemclemalitz (known as ClemClem) to build a church here. The first wooden building was completed in 1866. Later, using limestone blocks quarried from the hill, he built a more permanent church, which stands to this day. It is known as the Butter Church because it was financed in part from the sale of butter from parishioners' small farms. Services were held here for 10 years, but Rondeault's bishop thought the church should stand outside the reserve, so Rondeault built

The "new" Oblate mission church of St. Ann's, rebuilt in 1903 in heady Gothic style, replaced the earlier stone church on the nearby Cowichan reserve. It and its enormous graveyard are still in use.

another church, St. Ann's, just up the road, and services were held here from 1880. No longer consecrated, the lovely old Butter Church sits abandoned and vandalized, its doors and windows open to the elements and the prying fingers of wild blackberries.

A steep, stepped pathway leads up to the church a short distance north of the bridge. There's a small parking lot under the cliff. ClemClem, reportedly the largest of several First Nation villages on the Cowichan estuary, had 10 houses here in 1912.

About two kilometres north along the road, the "new" St. Ann's church, with its seemingly top-heavy steeple and large, well-populated graveyard, is not the church that Father Rondeault built. The original burned down in 1902 and was replaced by the present building a year later. Just beyond, at the end of a long lane, is red-roofed Providence Farm, established in 1864 by the Sisters of St. Ann as a farm and residential school, primarily for local First Nations children. No longer a school, the land is still being farmed by a community-owned organization that employs people with disabilities in the flower and vegetable gardens, orchard, furniture shop and other enterprises. There's a farm store and a kitchen where Providence-brand jams, jellies and preserves are made. Stop here for lunch and take a self-guided farm tour. It's a wonderful place to visit.

The original St. Ann's was known as the Butter Church because it was built in part with funds from pioneer farm butter sales. Built in 1866, this lovely old church stands derelict.

The slopes of Mount Tzouhalem rise up behind the church and the farm. Part of the Nature Conservancy's Mount Tzouhalem Ecological Reserve, the 40-hectare Chase Woods is an intact old forest of coastal Douglas fir and Garry oak meadows. The land includes limestone cliffs—home to nesting peregrine falcons—and the huge white landmark cross, erected on the summit by early missionaries. The woodland meadows are awash in wildflowers in April and May; the displays of blue camas are particularly beautiful.

Beyond Providence Farm, Tzouhalem Road meets the edge of the Duncan suburbs. Here, another old church, St. Peter's Anglican, was built on the site of the original Quamichan mission in 1876. Its heritage graveyard, where many local pioneers are buried (the earliest gravestones date from 1866), is shaded by old Oregon ash and Garry oak trees. The spring wildflowers here—blue camas, white erythroniums, pink shooting stars and chocolate lilies—bring botanists and photographers from afar. The church is easily found by following signs from Maple Bay Road to Church Road.

Turn right from Tzouhalem Road onto Maple Bay Road, which grazes the eastern edge of Quamichan Lake, a well-known wildlife reserve. Along here is Penfold Farm, a 1920s dairy farm with old barns and a creamery set amid flowery grounds. It is open for accommodation and garden tours. Nearby is the Nature Conservancy's Cowichan Garry Oak Preserve. While its native flora is being restored, the reserve is off limits; the trees and flowers can only be seen from an elevated viewing platform reached by a fenced walkway off Maple Bay Road. Just before the village of Maple Bay, a side road leads eight kilometres down to Genoa Bay, near the northern mouth of Cowichan Bay. This road hugs the shoreline of Birds Eye Cove, with its yacht club and

Both the Cowichan Garry Oak Preserve and Mount Tzouhalem Ecological Reserve have wonderful displays of spring wildflowers, including carpets of blue camas.

marinas, before diving into forests for the rest of the way to Genoa Bay village, a pretty waterfront community in a country setting with a store, cafe, art gallery and several docks crowded with boats and floathomes.

From Maple Bay, turn left onto Herd Road, a pleasantly hilly, twisty and rural route. There are several choices of roads north (if you're headed for Crofton, take Osborne Bay Road), but this route drives all the way west to Mays Road, one of the most idyllic country roads imaginable. Along this narrow, rollicking lane are mossy barns, a blueberry farm, a garden selling squash and sunflowers, a cattle ranch, meadows with sheep and goats, and a vineyard, all nicely bordered with old rail fences and tangled hedges of blackberry and snowberry and set against a backdrop of mountains. This is a road to walk rather than drive (or at least to drive slowly), and more than once. Mays Road dead-ends at Highway 1, but before it does so, it meets Bell McKinnon Road for a straight shot north to the curvier Westholme Road, which is bordered by more old farms and barns. This road becomes Chemainus Road (Highway 1A) as it winds through the Halalt First Nation reserve and then crosses the Chemainus River.

Chemainus is a small town whose livelihood since the 1860s has depended on the lumber industry. When the industry declined and the mills closed, Chemainus became a tourist mecca, but only because someone had the smart idea to transform the town into an art walk of history—giant murals were painted on every available wall, depicting scenes of past eras. Soon busloads of visitors were coming to gawk

and staying to appreciate the lively little streets full of Victorian cottages, shops, an active theatre and old wharves. Kinsmen Beach Park is a good place to watch both sunsets and sunrises. Small ferries cross the Strait of Georgia to Thetis and Kuper islands.

Chemainus Road continues north through the community of Saltair and rides close to the shore for several kilometres before merging with Highway 1 for the ride into Ladysmith, a town that sits smack dab on the 49th parallel. (The boundary line, which follows the 49th parallel religiously through the rest of British Columbia, deviates south to include the whole of Vancouver Island and some of the islands in the Gulf of Georgia.) Founded in 1899 as the town of Oyster Harbour because of rich oyster beds in the bay, Ladysmith was planned as an international port for shipments of coal from nearby mines and as a dormitory for mine workers. Its name was changed after only a year to honour the successful siege of Ladysmith in the South African Boer War. When the mines petered out, lumber for a while fuelled the town economy, and when that, too, diminished, the town turned to tourism.

Ladysmith is a fine old Edwardian town, its main street (1st Avenue) of handsome brick heritage buildings spruced up with tubs of flowers and historic markers. One of the hotels, and two churches, were moved here by train from the old mining town of Wellington. The town has some interesting eateries (Ladysmith is still known for its oysters) and offers accommodations. Across the highway, there's a beach park, marina, art gallery and a floating museum where, in summer, one can tour the harbour in a vintage wooden boat—a pleasant finale to the day's explorations. ❖

8

NORTH ISLAND CONNECTIONS

Along Vancouver Island's east coast, the mountains north of Campbell River descend almost down to the sea, their old bones wrapped in mists and swaddled with patchwork quilts of forest green. The first European settlers came here by boat and looked to the sea for their livelihood, not to the land. They were fishermen and cleared only garden plots on the narrow coastal plain. Later they relied mainly on the logging industry for sustenance, and logging still governs the North Island economy. Before Highway 19 was built to Sayward in 1978 and extended north to Port Hardy a year or so later, the only land access to communities along the north coast was by way of a rough, active logging track leading north from Gold River. This unpaved road was necessarily slow, all 65 kilometres of it, forcing travellers to take a long look at the rainforest in various stages of logging, from clear-cut to successfully replanted. They could see first-hand the difference between old forest and the second growth that came later. This gravel route provided total immersion, either dusty or muddy, into the deep green heartland of the island. In contrast, Highway 19 can be driven at a fair clip, so that the forests on either side whip by in a flash of green. Many visitors drive the highway non-stop to reach the Port Hardy ferry for transport north to Prince Rupert, but there is much to encourage a more leisurely approach.

This country road journey through the forests of the North Island diverges from the highway to travel some of the side roads that go deeper into the forest—roads meant to be driven at a slower pace, for they are, or were, logging roads, and few are paved. They lead to small coastal communities where fishing and logging, while both currently in decline, are still the major sources of income, though tourism is making inroads. Most of these branch roads must be travelled on a there-and-back basis, simply because there is no other access, except by boat.

The road to Zeballos crosses through Vancouver Island's thickly forested heart from east to west, providing lovely mountain views and reflections in Atluck Lake.

ferry to
Prince Rupert

Port Hardy

Beaver Harbour

Fort Rupert (Tsaxis)

Coal Harbour

MALCOLM ISLAND

route

community

park

ferry

place of interest ★

Port McNeil

CORMORANT ISLAND

Telegraph Cove

★**Beaver Cove**

Johnstone Strait

Nimpkish Lake

KELSEY BAY ★

Sayward

Eve River

Adam River

Bonanza Lake

NIMPKISH PARK

Highway 19

Salmon River

White River

Port Alice

to
Campbell
River

Little Huston Lake and Caves

Nimpkish River

Woss

SCHOEN LAKE PARK

WHITE RIVER PROVINCIAL PARK ★

Fair Harbour

WOSS LAKE PARK

To Gold River

Kyuquot

Zeballos

NORTH VANCOUVER ISLAND

North of Campbell River, Vancouver Island is separated from the mainland by a bewildering maze of islands and inlets so close together that it is hard to see just where a navigable passage lies. It's an infamous stretch of coastline, not only because of the narrow and tortuous channels, but for the winds and riptides that roar through—and, until fairly recently, for Ripple Rock, a twin-towered obstruction in Seymour Narrows on which many a ship foundered, and where at least 114 people have been lost. In 1958, Ripple Rock was taken out. Miners tunnelled under the seabed from Maud Island, off the coast of Quadra Island, to plant dynamite and set off one of the largest non-nuclear explosions in history. Ripple Rock was demolished, and ships plying the

Inside Passage now have a far safer route to navigate. A rest area off the highway just north of Campbell River provides a viewpoint of the scenic narrows where Ripple Rock used to be.

From here, the highway cuts inland from the coast and follows the Salmon River down to its junction with the White River, where a small pocket of agricultural land, a few straggly hay-fields and an old barn reveal the remains of an attempt at farming this wet and stony land. At this river junction (60 kilometres north of Campbell River), a paved road leads to the village of Sayward on the western edge of the Salmon's deep estuary. Originally known as Port Kusam for the First Nation community and mountain here, it was established as a coastal logging village in 1890 and renamed for William Sayward, a prominent Victoria pioneer who never even saw the place. A gravel road was put through from Campbell River during the Second World War, and, in 1978, the road was paved when the B.C. government started its northern ferry service from Kelsey Bay, just beyond the village. When the terminus was later moved up-Island to Port Hardy and the ferry traffic was diverted, Sayward lapsed back into a sleepy village still dependent on logging. From the old ferry dock, there's a fine view of Hkusam Mountain across the estuary, its sharp peak usually circled in mists. To local First Nations, this cloud effect formed a ring of steam "where the breath of the sea lion gathers at the blowhole."

Sayward Road crosses the Salmon River on a one-way bridge, beside which is the Cable Cook House, a popular restaurant that features a unique example of recycling: it is wrapped in 2,700 metres of logging cable. The river estuary is a wildlife reserve and a prime winter habitat for waterfowl; boardwalk trails lead here from the village. The river itself used to provide the Island's biggest steelhead, although the fishery is now partly closed to allow stocks to replenish. However, the fly-fishing here for Dolly Varden and cutthroat trout is good.

White River Provincial Park, reached by 25 kilometres of logging road, is home to a stand of huge ancient red cedars and Douglas firs, and all the jungled wealth of an almost untouched rain-forest floor. This 68-hectare wilderness park provides a glimpse of what all the original forest on the eastern slopes of Vancouver Island was like—mossy and tangled with ferns, with trees so tall their tops are often lost in the mist. How did this patch of heritage first-growth escape logging? It seems that in 1970, when fallers were sent from Kelsey Bay to harvest the trees, they found the site too beautiful to cut and persuaded the logging company to leave it intact. In 1994 word of this relict forest reached the film industry, and a crew arrived to shoot scenes for the period movie *The Scarlet Letter*. A few remnants of the film set remain here, the most visible (and useful) being sections of boardwalk that were constructed for horse-drawn carriages to rumble over. From the parking lot, a short loop trail leads down to the river through all those incredible trees. One Douglas fir tops out at more than 90 metres. The area is a prime habitat for Roosevelt elk and black bear, and, like most rivers here, the White offers good trout fishing.

To find the way to the park (there are few, if any, signs), go west across the highway at the Sayward junction and over the White River bridge. Immediately turn right onto Hern Road and right again onto Salmon River Main. Just past this intersection, watch for a road angling sharply uphill on your left. This is the White River Main. Keep going along this active logging road for almost 18 kilometres, then turn onto Victoria Main at a sharp U-bend. (If you cross the river for a second time, you have gone too far.) The provincial park boundary is six kilometres farther, and a small sign indicates old-growth access. Park here and enjoy a walk into an almost pristine rainforest nicknamed "The Cathedral Grove of the North Island." A word of caution: when active logging is taking place on these forest roads, it is advisable to limit your explorations to weekends. Cell phone service is, at best, limited.

About halfway between Campbell River and Port McNeill, Highway 19 meets the Nimpkish River and the small logging hamlet of Woss, a short distance west of the highway across the river bridge. The Nimpkish Valley was once the stronghold of the 'Namgis First Nation, who believe that their supernatural ancestor created the river, known to them as Gwa'ni, and filled it with salmon so they would never go hungry. The tribe controlled the main route through the valley connecting the east coast to the west coast, a trail known as the Eulachon or Grease Trail, since eulachon oil was one of the main trade commodities carried over it. This historic trail, recently re-established by the 'Namgis, starts from the head of Woss Lake, crosses a low divide and reaches tidewater in Tahsis Inlet. It has become a popular, if rugged, hiking trail, marked by tribal emblems carved on trees: a thunderbird at the east end and a wolf on the west. The 'Namgis village, which was originally at the mouth of the river, enters the history books as Cheslakee,

Hard to reach along dusty logging roads, tiny White River Provincial Park protects a stand of huge heritage first-growth trees that loggers from Kelsey Bay refused to cut.

96

the name of the chief who met with Captain Vancouver when his ship anchored offshore in 1792. When a fish cannery opened at Alert Bay on Cormorant Island across from the village, the 'Namgis decided to relocate to be closer to the jobs (see Chapter 12). Cheslakee village was virtually abandoned.

The thick woodlands of the Nimpkish Valley provided an early target for Island loggers, who moved in, set up camps, hacked roads and built railways—and steadily removed nearly all of the first-growth timber. But a small island in the river southwest of Woss escaped the axe; now Nimpkish River Ecological Reserve, the island shelters 18 hectares of 800-year-old first-growth forest, including Canada's tallest Douglas firs. It can only be accessed with a government permit.

Once the forests were cleared, most of the early logging railways were dismantled, but in the Nimpkish Valley, along the 100 kilometres of track from Vernon Camp to tidewater at Beaver Harbour,

The First Nations presence is strong in the Nimpkish Valley and along the north coast. This Kwakwaka'wakw figure is in Tsaxis village, near Fort Rupert.

logs are still hauled by rail. The line crosses the highway on overpasses at several places north of Woss. Today's trains on this largest private railway in Canada are pulled by diesel engines, but the rail yards at Woss display one of the old-timers, steam locomotive Number 113, which dates from 1920 and has been fully restored to working condition. The main logging road south from Woss to Gold River provides an alternate return trip south for those who don't mind gravel roads and occasional encounters with logging trucks.

Just north of Woss, a gravel road leads southwest 40 kilometres to the small community of Zeballos, at the head of Zeballos Inlet on the west coast. The road crosses the Nimpkish River and passes the turning to Little Huson Cave Regional Park, still listed on maps and signs as Hustan, though the caves were originally named for Alden Huson, who started a fish cannery at Alert Bay. Official changes to the name are being made. Here, in limestone karst

Zeballos, at the head of a deep inlet, was originally a mining centre, and the small heritage village retains its ambience. Today it's a fishing village, its harbour always full of boats.

The last of the logging railways, this, the largest private line in Canada, still hauls logs down the Nimpkish Valley to tidewater at Beaver Cove.

of the Quatsino Formation, which is extensive on Vancouver Island, spectacular caves and rock formations lie in unspoiled forest beside Little Huson Lake. The main cave's entrance is huge and can safely be explored without a guide. Just bring a good flashlight. Other caves include Vanishing River Cave and the Eternal Fountain.

To continue to Zeballos, keep generally south, following the road signs up to a low pass, then tracking the Zeballos River to tidewater. It's a good gravel road through second-growth forest, with some astonishing mountain views over Atluck Lake and across to spidery Mason Falls. It passes Zeballos' cemetery in the woods (planted with daffodils for a spring display) and a good viewpoint above the town, where a few mining relics set the stage for a history lesson. Like many places along the west coast, Zeballos Inlet was named by Spanish explorers: Captain Alejandro Malaspina sailed this way in 1792 in search of gold and put the Spanish imprint everywhere he could, naming this inlet after his lieutenant, Ciriaco Cevallos. The name was later interpreted as Zeballos. The Spanish did find gold here and elsewhere along the coast, as old documents testify: almost a million dollars in placer gold was shipped to Spain before the British took over. Later prospectors sniffing around the old workings in the mountains above the inlet found gold that the Spanish had missed. A minor stampede in the 1920s saw 40 claims registered, and 10 years later gold was still being taken from mines such as White Star and Golden Gate. The mining camp of Zeballos boomed. By 1938 the gold was being turned into bullion and shipped down the inlet, some $13 million worth altogether before the mines petered out. Population dwindled and the town might have disappeared altogether if logging and fishing had not come to the rescue.

Sheltered Beaver Cove is the main sorting ground for Nimpkish Valley logs, brought in by train and truck.

Today's small heritage village with its wooden buildings and boardwalks still faintly recalls the frenzy of gold-rush days, though the gold is long gone and the main historic anchor of the place, the 1938 Zeballos Hotel, has burned down. A modern replacement provides the same amenities, but not the romantic ambience. The townsite was built between the several outlet streams of the Zeballos River, and the side streets are bordered with ditches and awash in greenery. The whole estuary is now a wetlands reserve. From the Sugarloaf Bridge, across the main channel, one can watch salmon spawning in the fall, and the eagles and bears that join the fracas. Trumpeter swans and hordes of gulls are also here, on the hunt for salmon eggs, along with great blue herons. If you decide to stay a while for kayak explorations or hikes to old mine sites, there's very good food in the Blue Heron Restaurant at the Cedars Inn, the refurbished old hospital.

For the intrepid, a long unpaved road staggers some 35 rough kilometres across the mountains from Zeballos to Fair Harbour, where there is only a government dock, a boat launch and a few campsites. Kayakers launch their boats here to explore the wilderness coastlines of Kyuquot Sound and Checleset Bay, where the steep mountain slopes are covered with virgin stands of huge Sitka spruce—the only trees able to survive the frequent lashings of salt spindrift from the battering storms. Checleset Bay has been successfully repopulated with sea otters, transported here from the Aleutian Islands. From an initial immigration of 300, otter numbers have increased to more than 2,000, and the animals have spread south into Barkley Sound. Fair Harbour is the closest road access to the fishing village of Kyuquot, one of the most remote communities on the west coast. Water taxi service can be arranged. The only

Telegraph Cove is an old fishing village with boardwalks and a fine harbour. It has become very popular as a centre for whale-watching trips.

other regular service to the village is on the MV *Uchuck III*, which makes weekly trips from Gold River (see Chapter 14).

Return to Highway 19 and continue north, following the Nimpkish River and tracking the long thin finger of Nimpkish Lake for 22 kilometres. The lake is popular with windsurfers, who come to play when strong northwesterlies blow. Accessing the lake is difficult: you can get to it only from the north and south ends, and at Kinman Creek Recreation Site, about halfway along.

Past the lake, the highway turns abruptly west. Instead, turn right here to Beaver Cove and on to the community once known as Huson's Cove (for the same Alden Huson who discovered the caves). Huson's Cove was renamed Telegraph Cove when it became the terminus of the first telegraph line on the North Island, and today Telegraph Cove is world-famous as a centre for whale-watching expeditions into Broughton and Johnstone straits. It is close to the Robson Bight Ecological Reserve, one of the few known places where orcas swim onto beach gravels for body rubs. The road to this popular village crosses the Kokish River and follows the bay around to Beaver Cove, the main log-sorting and booming ground at the end of the Nimpkish logging railway. A parking spot above the cove provides a good view of the action as huge machinery tosses logs about and tugboats manoeuvre among the booms. The rusting ghost of an old steam locomotive lies almost hidden in the forest nearby. Cross the logging railway and continue around to Telegraph Cove village.

In a way, the worldwide attraction of whale-watching and the accompanying hordes of people have spoiled some of the charm of what used to be a quiet little village built on stilts

Older Telegraph Cove homes were built on stilts over tidewater and connected by boardwalks. The walks now lead to B & Bs, restaurants, gift shops and a whale museum.

around the harbour and with a boardwalk main street. A huge resort has been built across the bay, with new wharves and berths for hundreds of boats, and large parking lots carved out of the forest. On the plus side, the new interest has brought survival: old dilapidated wooden buildings have been preserved and given a facelift of paint. It's still an attractively authentic place—albeit gentrified—with echoes of a simpler bygone age. Small cottages line the boardwalk: some are residences, while others have been converted into tourist rentals, shops, galleries or restaurants such as the Killer Whale Cafe and the Old Saltery Pub, a new building constructed from reworked lumber from the 1920s saltery. Each building bears a plaque describing its age, former purpose and the name of the original occupant, so that the whole village seems to be a living museum. The actual museum is devoted to whales, with gigantic skeletons hanging from the rafters and well-displayed educational exhibits. Telegraph Cove may be overcommercialized, but it's well worth a visit. It's also home base to some of the best whale-watching and ocean discovery trips on the coast.

Return to the highway, cross the broad Nimpkish River close to its estuary and continue north into Port McNeill, a logging town since 1938, when fire destroyed most of the forests on Malcolm Island just offshore; the logging camps' floathomes on Malcolm Island were simply ferried across and anchored in Port McNeill's bay. Today Port McNeill is the civic hub of the North Island, with schools, a hospital and government offices. With its large docks, marinas and ferry links, it is also fast becoming a tourist town, with a reputation for some of the best scuba diving anywhere. The harbourfront has a pleasant promenade and wharves full of colourful fishboats. Ferries leave from here for Malcolm and Cormorant islands (see Chapter 12). Back on Highway 19, stop to admire the 22-ton burl that was found growing at the base of a 350-year-old spruce and hauled here to mark the west entrance to town.

Vancouver Island narrows as it reaches its northern tip, and deep inlets and sounds reach inland from the west coast, almost separating the island into a jigsaw puzzle of smaller islands and making the land very difficult to access, even from the sea. It was by sea that traders of the Hudson's Bay Company arrived when they heard that coal was being mined here on the northeast coast by local First Nations. They investigated and started a mine of their own at Suquash, just up the coast from Port McNeill, and in 1849 the company built Fort Rupert in nearby Beaver Harbour, the nearest sheltered port for deep-sea ships. Local Kwakwaka'wakw people left their villages along the Cluxewe River and moved close to the fort, where they built a row of cedar houses along the shore outside the fort palisades. Soon their new village of Tsaxis had a population of several thousand and was, for a while, the largest metropolis on the North Island.

This early mine was a disappointment. Unlike the rich bituminous beds found later near Nanaimo, it produced only poor-quality coal. There were other problems, too. The

The First Nation village of Tsaxis, south of Port Hardy, retains its traditions. The Big House has a handsomely decorated facade featuring the two-headed monster Sisiutl. The Hunt family's Copper Maker Gallery is here.

Kwakwaka'wakw, arguing that the land and the coal was theirs, demanded payment. Then the fort burned and had to be rebuilt. In 1882 the Hudson's Bay mines were shut down, and the Fort Rupert store was turned over to the incumbent factor, Robert Hunt, whose wife, Mary, was a Tlingit noblewoman. The Hunts had 11 children, the beginning of the Hunt dynasty of artists, carvers and dancers, which is still dominant. The fort itself later burned down again; one lone brick chimney, almost lost in bushes and brambles, is all that remains, but the village of Tsaxis is still there. Its long main street curves around the shore of the island-dotted bay and centres around the community Big House, a huge weathered grey cedar box, with a three-dimensional Sisiutl, or two-headed serpent, sprawled across its face. There is a weedy but wonderful graveyard (complete with totems), a decorated school, carved cedar canoes in a boat shed and other indications of a still-thriving indigenous culture. The Hunt family is still there: Calvin and Marie Hunt run the Copper Maker Gallery, which has a fine collection of original art prints, carvings and jewellery upstairs and a carving studio on the lower level.

The Fort Rupert coal mines were reopened in 1908 and were worked sporadically for the next 30 years. At the start of the Second World War, the largest airfield on the North Island was built on land next to the village as home base for RCAF Station Port Hardy, which operated here from 1939 until the end of the war. The airport still operates, but is now for civilian use. The terminal building sports some grand totems.

To reach the ruins of Fort Rupert, take Byng Road toward Port Hardy airport, south of the town, turn left onto Beaver Harbour Road, then right onto Tsakis Road, the main village thoroughfare. The chimney of the Hudson's Bay fort, the oldest European building on the Island's north coast, is easily missed. At the south end of the village, just past a tiny church and the general store, cross a small bridge and immediately look for the historic remains in the forest on the left side. It is well worth returning to Beaver Harbour Road, continuing north to the ballpark and turning there onto Storey's Beach Road, which parallels the north shoreline of the protected bay—a wonderful area to watch shorebirds at low tide.

Port Hardy, the largest settlement on the North Island, marks the end of Highway 19 and the beginning of ferry service north through the Inside Passage. It was settled in 1904 when a splinter group from the Fort Rupert Hunt family opened a store here for fishermen. More settlers arrived eight years later in response to glowing advertisements placed in English and American newspapers by the Hudson's Bay Company in an effort to sell off their lands. The small fishing and lumber town grew slowly because of its isolation. Always reliant on resource extraction, it has endured a long history of boom and bust; the logging and fishing industries are in decline, and the nearby copper mine, once the largest open-pit operation in the world, shut down in 1996. Today, Port Hardy looks to tourism as a major lifeline, and it is well situated for wildlife touring, hiking and exploration: huge Cape Scott, one of the world's premier wilderness destinations, sits at its doorstep. In town, there's a pleasant sea walk from Market Street to Hardy Bay, and the heritage Seagate Hotel is still in business by the old Government Wharf.

It's only a 20-minute drive (15 kilometres) from Port Hardy to the west-coast destination of Coal Harbour, a small village at the junction of Holberg and Rupert inlets. It was founded, as it name suggests, when coal was discovered here in 1883 and a group of Norwegians struggled overland from Port Hardy to start a settlement. They called it Scandia, then changed the name to Quatsino and later to Coal Harbour. The Northwest Coal Company worked the mines for a while, but the coal was poor and the company closed shop, leaving a caretaker to guard the premises. His name was John Sharp, and his background was obscure. In 1907 two men slipped into the area and murdered him. There were rumours that John Sharp was an alias for one of

Port Hardy, at the end of Highway 19, is home to the ferry terminal for Prince Rupert and points north. Fishermen still unload their catch at the Government Wharf and call in at the historic Seagate Hotel.

Jesse James' gang of bank robbers, and that he had loot stashed away at the mine site. The murderers—and the loot, if any—were never found.

In 1920 a road was put through from Port Hardy, and Coal Harbour lived on, sustained by fishing and logging. But, in 1940, it became an RCAF seaplane base, with barracks for 250 personnel and a fleet of long-range flying boats that patrolled offshore, defending Canada against enemy attack. (All that came was a single incendiary balloon, designed to ignite forest fires; it fell near Holberg with no reported damage.) After the war, the town took on yet another new persona as a whaling port, and several of the airmen stayed on to participate. From 1948 until 1967, Coal Harbour whalers killed and processed some 4,000 whales. It was the largest (and the last) whaling station on the B.C. coast, and it closed only when whale stocks seriously diminished. The large open-pit copper mine that sustained Port Hardy helped Coal Harbour too for a while, but that also closed.

Today the village has fallen back onto fishing, logging and aquaculture, with tourism as its brightest hope. There's not too much to see in the village, except perhaps the huge jawbones of a blue whale, seven metres high and mounted for display, but the maritime view down the inlet, enfolding mountains of differing shades of blue, is beautiful. To reach the site of the RCAF station, with its barracks and a huge hangar for the planes, turn right along a gravel road at the start of the Government Wharf. Opposite the hangar, an RCAF flag still flaps above the waterfront near a memorial to the airmen lost in service here. An old cannon commemorates the whaling days.

The easy return route retraces Highway 19 south to Campbell River. An alternative route is the forest road from Woss to Gold River—and Gold River is the start of another adventure (see Chapter 14). ❧

9

OLD ROAD, CREATIVE ISLANDS

From Qualicum Beach all the way north to Campbell River, Vancouver Island's old road, Highway 19A, is the route to follow, not only to drive closer to the shore, but to enjoy the small settlements and their gentler pace of life. Halfway along the route lie the islands of Denman and Hornby (reached by ferries), where country roads connect with the vibrant creative spirit of the islanders—potters, painters, weavers, sculptors, jewellery makers—as well as growers of fruits, vegetables, wines and flowers. If you want to see island creativity at its best, visit the farmers' and craft markets, or take a summer art-studio tour.

Qualicum Beach is one of the older holiday villages on the east coast of the Island, and summers are busy here. Its fine scenery and mild weather were noted by explorers as early as 1864, and the first settlers arrived by boat a few years later. A wagon road from Nanaimo was cut through the forest a few years later, but it was only when the E & N Railway arrived from Victoria that the settlement became popular for summer vacations. The village keeps the flavour of an English beachside resort. Here, a combination of tides and currents and a gently sloping shoreline have created wide stretches of sandy beach where the water becomes tropically warm as the sea creeps in over sun-hot sand. The village takes good care of its history: the 1914 railway station has been restored, and there's an old steam locomotive and freight shed nearby; the art gallery is housed in the two-storey 1912 schoolhouse and the museum in the 1929 brick power-house. On display here, in addition to pioneer memorabilia, is a fine collection of fossils, one of the largest in western Canada.

Gardeners will admire the floral displays—the village regularly wins the Communities in Bloom contest—and they will want to set aside time to visit nearby Milner Gardens. On the Gardens' clifftop bluff, a large tract of first-growth cedar and Douglas fir forest has been

Both Denman and Hornby islands are known for their artists and craftspeople, but there are also many small farms and market gardens and lots of roadside stands.

preserved around a 1928 heritage house where British royalty were once entertained. The manicured gardens are noted for their botanical variety, with spring displays of rhododendrons and camellias, and rare trees and shrubs. Dainty English teas are served in the drawing room on summer afternoons.

Highway 19A is mostly two lanes wide and winding—sometimes right along the beachfront, sometimes in forest shade with only occasional glimpses of the shore. A few kilometres north of Qualicum Beach, a well-marked side road leads to Horne Lake Caves Provincial Park, where guided tours provide underworld journeys through caverns and tunnels full of crystalline formations thousands of years old. Underground waterfalls, streams and canyons, with fossils of crinoids, ancient sea creatures older than dinosaurs, can be viewed in these caves. Two of them

*Fanny Bay in
Baynes Sound
is famous for its
oysters. Don't stop
at this roadside
display, though:
its products are for
sale by the Denman
ferry dock.*

are open for self-guided tours; the longer Riverbend Cave can only be seen with a guide. The caves are natural—there is no lighting or boardwalk—and are reached by a short forest trail and suspension bridge across the Qualicum River.

Past the small settlement of Bowser, turn right to drive to Deep Bay, where a marina is tucked behind the hook of Mapleguard Point. It's a picturesque bay, full of fishboats. Here, tiny nesting boxes on wharf pilings house a large colony of purple martins. These birds, never very common along the southern B.C. coast, suffered a serious decline in numbers mainly because of habitat loss. In 1997 a solitary pair was seen nesting in a crevice on a Deep Bay piling. Naturalists put up nesting boxes here and at other locations, including Cowichan and Oyster bays, and each year the number of martins has increased. The birds, which resemble large dark swallows, swoop and twitter among the fishboats. The outer edge of Deep Bay looks across to the southern tip of Denman Island and tiny Chrome Island, with its lighthouse and cluster of red buildings.

The shallow waters and intertidal beaches of protected Baynes Sound provide ideal conditions for spawning herring. In March the offshore waters here turn milky blue green as huge schools of fish arrive to deposit their eggs and milt. Each female lays 30,000 eggs onto kelp or algae, eggs that are prime food for swooping, screeching flocks of gulls, eagles and herons. The feeding frenzy lasts for days. B.C.'s herring boats also swing into action; the fish they catch are frozen, the eggs stripped from the females for processing and the carcasses made into pet food or fertilizer. While this fishery is controlled, it attracts much criticism and there is active lobbying

for a gentler form of roe collection in which the fish are captured, allowed to spawn, then returned alive to the sea. Local Coast Salish used to gather at the shore for "chummish," lowering branches of cedar or hemlock into the shallows for the females to lay their eggs on. After awhile, the branches would be retrieved and the roe stripped off and dried for winter use.

Baynes Sound is also famous for oysters, which are raised commercially both on the beach and on trays suspended in the ocean. Pioneer oysterman Joseph McLellan noticed the prime shellfish conditions here and imported a load of seed oysters from Japan in the 1940s. These oysters, bigger than the native species, thrived, and so did the Manila clams that had hitched a ride with the immigrant shellfish. Today, Mac's Oysters, still in the hands of the McLellan family, ships oysters and clams to markets around the world. Oyster sprats are reared on giant netted bundles of glistening white oyster shells, heaps of which can be seen beside Mac's farm-gate store. Odd-looking shallow oyster boats bob offshore. Another company, Fanny Bay Oysters, sells its products at its seafood market beside the Buckley Bay ferry terminal.

North of Deep Bay, the highway cuts through Rosewall Creek Provincial Park, where the flats of Mud Bay provide prime winter habitat for shorebirds and waterfowl. Fanny Bay, north of Ship Peninsula, has become famous for more than its plump oysters. The commodious Fanny Bay Inn, known locally as the FBI, has a loyal following, both for its fine pub food and the view from its seaside deck.

The Denman Island ferry leaves from Buckley Bay, four kilometres north of Fanny Bay. If you plan to visit both Denman and Hornby islands (it is possible in one long day) take a through

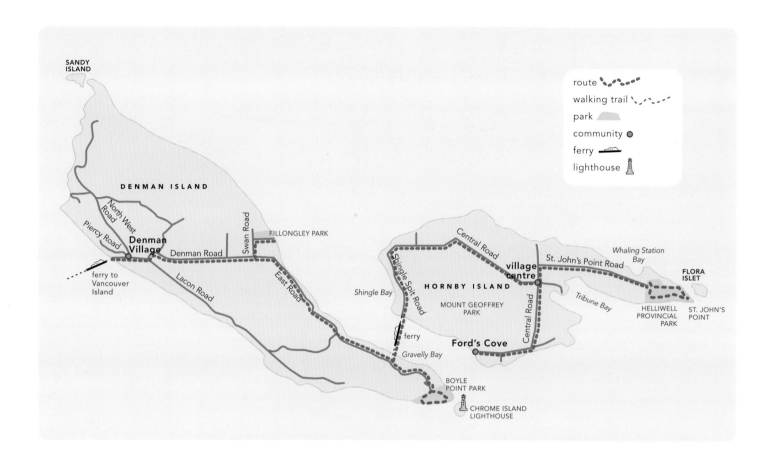

ticket (as with most small-island ferries, tickets are sold only on a return basis) and go first to Hornby, because the ferries are timed for an easy connection. Once on Denman, it is easy to get to the Hornby ferry: simply follow the main road (and most of the traffic) across the island to the Gravelly Bay terminal. It's only a short ride across the channel to Shingle Spit on Hornby Island. Near the dock is the Thatch Pub and restaurant, its roof thatched with living grass and wildflowers. The adjacent Visitor Centre provides copies of the Hornby Island Arts Council Studio Guide, which is not only a great road map, but also shows the locations of the more than 60 studios on the island. Some studios are open daily in summer (July and August) and others by appointment.

Head north along Shingle Spit Road to Phipps Point, where Central Road swings east across the island's rural heart, past Carbrea Vineyard & Winery and the Cardboard House bakery. The "downtown," dominated by the large Co-op Store and Ringside Craft Market, clusters around the intersection of Central and Sollans Road. The nearby sod-roofed Community Hall plays host to farmers' markets on Wednesdays and Saturdays. From the Co-op, continue south on Central Road, passing side roads to the expansive sandy beaches in Tribune Bay, then driving

A shady stroll through the forest at Denman Island's Boyle Point Park leads to a high lookout for an eagle-eye view of Chrome Island Lighthouse.

through second-growth forests on the slopes of Mount Geoffrey Escarpment Provincial Park. Turn uphill onto Strachan Road, and then make further turns onto Marylebone and Euston roads (apparently named after London railway stations) to visit Middle Mountain Meadery for artisan honey wine and splendid views.

Central Road ends abruptly at Ford's Cove Public Wharf, where the general store includes a gift gallery and small restaurant. It's a popular spot for kayaking and scuba diving—there are scuba supplies at the wharf —and glorious sunsets. In March, it's also a good place to watch the herring frenzy. Today an end-of-the-road small community, Ford's Cove is where European settlement on Hornby began. At the end of the 1860s, with the island's Pentlatch people annihilated by sickness or carried off in slave raids, a huge forest fire engulfed the deserted island. Seeing the flames and smoke from nearby Comox Harbour, pioneer George Ford decided to relocate here, since fires made land clearing far easier.

Other settlers followed, and in 1870, a whaling company moved to the island, pre-empting land at what is now Whaling Station Bay. It closed shop after two years for lack of whales, leaving nothing behind on the fine curving beach with its sandstone shelves, rock pools and sandy shallows. To reach Whaling Station Bay, return north up Central Road past "downtown" and then turn east onto St. John's Point Road. The bay is accessed from the end of several short spur roads between houses.

Don't miss a walk in Helliwell Provincial Park. Follow St. John's Point Road almost to its end, then turn onto Helliwell Road to a parking lot. From here, a five-kilometre forested trail

loops around high grassy bluffs that overlook rocky coves and inlets and are carpeted with wild-flowers in spring. It's a wonderful walk, even in stormy weather. Scuba divers favour the point because of the clear water and a wide diversity of undersea life, including the rare shallow-water appearance of the six-gill shark, a creature some five metres long, found around Flora Islet. Nearby is the underwater wreck of the HMS *Alpha*, capsized in 1900.

Return to Denman Island on the ferry, turn left on arrival at Gravelly Bay and head south to Boyle Point Provincial Park for another wonderful walk. A 20-minute stroll through the woods leads to a high headland and an eagle's eye view of the Chrome Island lighthouse, seemingly tethered by cables just offshore. Look for a prominent eagle's nest nearby, and scan for seals and sea lions on the rocks below. Head back to the ferry dock and drive north on East Road along the shore of Lambert Channel, where the pebble beaches are easily seen and accessed. Near the junction with Denman Road, Swan Road leads north to Fillongley Park, with its alluring sand and shell beach and stands of old-growth rainforest. Denman Village, where the ferry docks, is the island's commercial hub, anchored by the false-fronted general store that dates from 1910. Nearby are St. Saviour's Church (1914) and the farm market and museum in the huge 1875 barn on Piercy Road. There are artists' studios throughout the island, and much of their work can be seen at the Arts Denman Society's gallery. There's a lot happening on this small island: a Saturday market in the Old School, annual tours to pottery and art studios, a home and gardens tour, and a writer's festival.

A 10-minute ferry hop across Baynes Sound returns travellers to Highway 19A on Vancouver Island and the slow route to Campbell River. North from the ferry is Union Bay, once a busy coal port. Coal from nearby mines was transported by railway to a deep-sea wharf for export

Boyle Point Park preserves a large plot of tall heritage trees and wonderful ferny undergrowth. The easy loop trail is well marked.

The headlands at Helliwell Park on Hornby Island are open and grassy and traversed by a cliffside trail that meanders through stands of arbutus trees.

(at first by sailing ship) around the world. The first to call was the *San Mateo* in 1889, the same year that a post office opened here. Coke ovens were built in 1896, with bricks (and bricklayers) imported from Scotland. Maintenance shops for the locomotives, a machine shop, a blacksmith's shop and two large hotels, the Nelson (1895) and the Wilson (1898), were built. Workers' houses soon sprang up, and then a school, a church and a bank, and population swelled to 10,000. But the coal supply eventually dwindled. The last coal ship, the *Pamir*, sailed from Union Bay in 1946; the mines closed, and the community collapsed.

The railway and wharf have gone: all that is left of coal-mining days are the raised railbed, derelict wharf pilings, and a few heaps of coal and slag near the Washer Creek Bridge. But cheek by jowl alongside the highway are a few splendid relics of the pioneer townsite: the 1906 United Church, the huge old post office (1915), the house of the master mechanic (1911), and the tiny 1901 jail with its barred windows and lovely ornamental knot garden, lush with lavender, now a gift shop/museum. The buildings were preserved (and some of them moved into place) by the Union Bay Historical Society.

Union Bay has a fascinating tale to tell of Henry Wagner, the elusive "Flying Dutchman," and his gang, who raced up and down the coast in a fast and super-silent speedboat, docking in the dead of night and creeping ashore to rob and plunder. The burglars were hard to catch, because they were safely back at sea long before citizens woke to the fact that they had been robbed. But in 1913, the Flying Dutchman met his match. Alert police officers noticed a light in Fraser and Bishop's store at the end of the Union Bay wharf and decided to investigate. They were met with a fusillade of bullets. Officer Henry Westaway was killed, but Constable Gordon

Ross managed to overpower one of the robbers (it is said that his thumb was bitten off in the scuffle). The rest of the gang escaped, but Ross had luckily (and pluckily) collared the gang leader. Wagner was found guilty of murder and became the last man to be hanged in the city of Nanaimo in August 1913—swift justice. Other gang members were later found hiding out on Lasqueti Island. The Flying Dutchman sailed no more.

A short distance north is Royston, a community loosely spread out along the highway. Turn on Hayward Avenue toward the water onto Marine Drive and follow it along the bay's beachfront. At the northern end, pilings of another old dock—the end of a logging railway from the Comox Valley— now buttress a breakwater reinforced with the wrecks of old ships, everything from a wooden lumber schooner to massive iron boats and tugs. A storyboard along the waterfront walkway tells the history of these "ghost ships." At low tide, one can walk out to inspect the wrecks, now grown over with weeds and brambles. There are more purple martin nesting boxes on the pilings here.

A side trip to the coal-mining village of Cumberland, once the second-largest coal producer in North America, will take the traveller into the foothills by way of Royston and Dunsmuir roads. Founded in 1864, the town's heyday peaked between 1900 and 1914, when more than 13,000 people from all around the world worked here, including 1,500 Japanese and 3,000 Chinese. Its Chinatown, once the largest north of San Francisco, was destroyed by fire; the only relic is Jumbo's Cabin, later used as the office of the Union Coal Company. Amazingly, for a community that seriously declined with the mines in the 1920s and should have died when the last coal mine closed in the 1960s, Cumberland has kept many of its heritage buildings and is undergoing a revival as a quaint art town, as well as a venue for world-class mountain biking, hiking and

117

RIGHT *Vancouver Island's east coast is sheltered by offshore islands. Sunset near Buckley Bay brings gulls to the low-tide beaches.*

skiing in the Beaufort Range, at the edge of Strathcona Park. A walk along Cumberland's main street reveals its innovative survivor attitude. The 1907 Waverley Hotel is still in business. The museum provides guided tours and maps of the mine sites, as well as information on the tragic history of the mines, including the underground fires and explosions (nearly 300 miners were killed here) and a bitter two-year strike. Very close to the highway intersection on Union Street, the large Chinese and Japanese graveyards are as manicured as any park.

From Cumberland, return to Royston. The coastal road along the southern edge of deep Comox Harbour provides good views across the bay and pushes through the towns of Courtenay and Comox, which have grown together into a tangle of suburbs and big-box stores. The ski resort of Mount Washington, known for its deep and early snow, can be visited in summer for chairlift rides into the alpine meadows (wildflowers are profuse in Paradise Meadows in late June) and a multitude of mountain trails on Forbidden Plateau. Keep north on 19A through farmland to Merville and Black Creek, and make time for a visit to Miracle Beach Provincial Park, which has everything: forest trails, secluded campsites, a wide and wonderful sandy beach, tide pools and mountain views across the Strait of Georgia. Farther north, the road reaches Oyster Point and the large Oyster Bay Shoreline Park, where more old pilings house yet more martin nests. Northward, to Stories Beach, Shelter Point and Ocean Grove, the highway becomes a garden-edged drive with accessible beach all the way to Campbell River. Park the car and go for a stroll, enjoying the view across to the lighthouse on Quadra Island. Campbell River is a jumping-off point: from here you can head east via a ferry to Quadra Island (see Chapter 13), west to Gold River, or north to the up-Island communities of Sayward, Port McNeill and Port Hardy (see Chapter 8). ❧

OPPOSITE *Comox Harbour is wide and deep and well frequented by birdwatchers and kayakers. Flowers brighten the shore north of Royston.*

10

SALT SPRING PASTORALE

Salt Spring Island, the largest of a raft of little islands moored in the Strait of Georgia, has two ferry connections to Vancouver Island: one from Vesuvius Bay on the northwest part of the island, and one from Fulford Harbour in the south. A third ferry, from Long Bay, near Ganges, links the island to the Tsawwassen ferry terminal on the mainland. One can guess from these services that Salt Spring is not only the largest but also the most densely populated of the islands, though one would not know this from the look of the land. Once famous for its apples and still well known for its tender lamb, the island has a pastoral air, its green fields well nibbled by flocks of sheep.

Salt Spring is an artists' haven. Painters, potters, weavers, jewellery makers, woodworkers, glass-blowers and photographers have chosen the island lifestyle, and their studios are often open to the public. There are also vintners and cheese makers, garlic farmers, bread bakers, sheep farmers, lavender growers and orchardists. Tracking down all these homemade and home-grown delights gives travellers a fine excuse to explore the back lanes.

Between the three ferry landings, an intricate meander of country roads loops through the island, making it ideal for a leisurely day's drive. Most of the roads are narrow, closely edged by fences, hedgerows or tall trees; few have parking shoulders. Fifteen of them are designated heritage roads, named for the pioneers whose trails they follow, and hopefully these will never be widened, nor their twists and angles straightened out. A winding road, its delights hidden around unexpected corners, calls for slow travel with many stops. Be prepared to share these roads, particularly on weekends, with walkers and cyclists, horseback riders, dogs and even sheep!

Like other land along the coast, Salt Spring is geologically ancient, formed about 400 million years ago near present-day Australia, part of a volcanic archipelago that slowly drifted

From the high cliffs atop Mount Maxwell, the green fields of Salt Spring Island lead the eye down to the shore at Fulford Harbour and across to myriad misty islands.

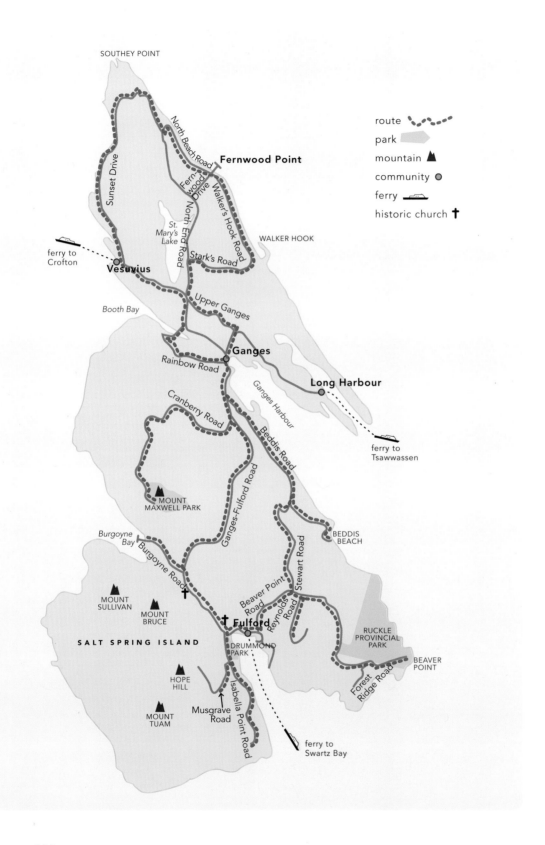

SOUTHEY POINT

North Beach Road

Fernwood Point

Sunset Drive

Fernwood Drive

North End Road

Walker's Hook Road

St. Mary's Lake

WALKER HOOK

ferry to Crofton

Vesuvius

Stark's Road

Upper Ganges

Booth Bay

Rainbow Road

Ganges

Ganges Harbour

Long Harbour

Cranberry Road

Beddis Road

ferry to Tsawwassen

MOUNT MAXWELL PARK

Ganges-Fulford Road

BEDDIS BEACH

Burgoyne Bay

Burgoyne Road

Stewart Road

MOUNT SULLIVAN

MOUNT BRUCE

Beaver Point Road

Reynolds Road

Fulford

RUCKLE PROVINCIAL PARK

BEAVER POINT

SALT SPRING ISLAND

DRUMMOND PARK

HOPE HILL

Isabella Point Road

Musgrave Road

MOUNT TUAM

Forest Ridge Road

ferry to Swartz Bay

route

park

mountain ▲

community ◉

ferry 🚢

historic church †

north and east as the Pacific Ocean rift was pushed apart. Some of the islands were later intruded by volcanic magma, and others became surrounded by coral reefs, which turned gradually into limestone. The resulting conglomerate of drifting rock is known to geologists as the Wrangellia Terrane. Its 10,000-kilometre journey to collision point and eventual adhesion with the intractable North American continent took 300 million years. Since then, Wrangellia, which underpins much of Vancouver Island, the Gulf Islands and parts of the mainland, has been overlaid by sand and shale laid down in shallow seas, then drowned in glacial ice, which scoured out the major valleys. Traces of this tumultuous past can be read in the rocks, on beaches and headlands, in road cuts and mountaintops. Compared to geologic time, the entire human history of the island happened only yesterday.

Evidence of human occupation of Salt Spring Island dates back

Daisies spangle the shady grass at Drummond Park, across from the village of Fulford.

almost 5,000 years, dates confirmed by archaeologists who uncovered traces of settlement along the shore at places such as Ganges, Long Harbour and Hudson Point. Decimation by disease and intertribal warfare led to shifts in island populations, and, by the 1800s, only a few First Nations people remained on the island. They were eventually allotted the small Tsawout reserve, today unoccupied, near Fulford Harbour.

The first outsiders to settle here were nine black former slaves, part of a group of 600 colonists brought to B.C. from California by the Hudson's Bay Company, which had been ordered to place colonists here, not only to satisfy the terms of their Crown lease, but to strengthen Britain's territorial claims. The group was promised free passage, free land, and, best of all, freedom from slavery. The nine chose Salt Spring Island, and they settled here in 1857. During the homesteading years from 1850 to 1900, immigrants arrived from many countries and the island valleys became a checkerboard of small holdings, many of them sheep farms and apple orchards nestled under the protective slopes of quite high, forested mountains. The island still has more than 200 small farms, an amazing number, given that only a small percentage of the land is arable, though the climate is kind. Caught in the double rain shadow of the Vancouver Island and Olympic Peninsula mountains, Salt Spring is dry and warm.

The island divides naturally into three sections—on a map, it looks as if three small humpy islands decided to stick together. The northern section has the most arable land and the biggest lake: St. Mary's. On the east coast of the island, the Hudson's Bay Company discovered the cold briny springs that gave the island its name. (Is it Salt Spring, or Saltspring? Most maps—and most locals—prefer the original two-word name, but the latter spelling is the officially correct one.) The central section of the island is riven by a large U-shaped valley, which accommodated both the early settlers and the backbone of the island's road system. The island's southern bulge is dominated by a huge, forested mountain massif now protected as part of the Gulf Islands National Park Reserve.

This island journey begins where the first colonists arrived, at Vesuvius Bay (named for a British warship), where ferries from Crofton on Vancouver Island nose regularly into the dock. The road leading uphill from the terminal is often choked with ferry traffic, and the friendly general store and neighborhood pub—a replica replacement of the first inn, built in 1873 by Portuguese sailor Estalon Bittancourt—are always busy. Beside the dock, a tiny Catholic chapel is now an arts and crafts gallery.

At the top of the hill from the ferry, turn a sharp left (north) along Sunset Drive, named for the often flamboyant sunsets enjoyed from this part of the island. It's a comfortable country road, with a few old barns, flocks of sheep and munching cows in the fields alongside. Watch for Sunset Farm with its flock of Romney sheep and a store selling different kinds of sheep-ish

A rocky cove at Southey Point (at the north end of Salt Spring) provides anchorage for small boats and a view of the clear blue water.

items, including fleece, raw wool and knitting yarns. At the junction with Southey Point Road (ironically, near the island's northern tip), the Jack Foster Trail leads to a wide and lonely pebble beach, covered with shells. Other rights-of-way (at the ends of Arbutus and Southey Point roads) provide access to smaller beaches with tidal pools and eroded sandstone shelves. Sunset Drive becomes North End Road and heads south along the island's eastern shore. Where this road divides, turn left onto North Beach Road, which hugs the shoreline, past the salt springs—now a spa—down to Fernwood Point. Here one can watch the antics of harbour seals from the public wharf and scan the horizon for whales. There is much of geologic interest here: the tidal flats north of the wharf feature beds of ancient shales, once mud, still bearing the tracks of small animals, and at Hudson Point there are eroded sandstone boulders and smoothed glacial erratics of granite, pushed here from the Coast Mountains.

Beyond the wharf, the road continues south as Walker's Hook Road, for this is where it goes, a finger of land that doubles back on itself, creating a deep narrow bay. The tidal flats in the shelter of the hook team with shore birds, gulls and eagles; access is at the foot of Grantville Street. Continue south, curving onto Stark's Road, named for one of the first black families. Sylvia Estes Stark arrived here when she was 21, lived to 105 and is buried in the Ganges graveyard. Continue on to Ganges by way of North End and Upper Ganges roads. Watch for St. Mark's Church (1892) and the Vesuvius Burial Ground, where most of the early settlers are laid to rest. The burial ground is located behind the 1898 Central Hall, once the community centre for the whole island.

Busy, busy Ganges is the largest and most fashionable Salt Spring community, though the pioneer Mouat's Trading Company general store still anchors the shopping action at the new Grace Point Square.

Skinny Athol Peninsula and the more muscular arm of Scott Point enclose the deep inlet of Long Harbour, where the ferry from the mainland arrives to unload its automobiles and passengers along the road to Ganges, which crowds the north end of another deep harbour. The largest village on the island, Ganges is an eclectic mix of slow island ways and smart tourist commercialism. In the centre of the action, Mouat's Trading Company, a great old-fashioned general store, albeit a bit gentrified, has been the heart of the community since it was built before the turn of the last century. Thomas and Jane Mouat came to Salt Spring from the Shetland Islands, and when Thomas died in 1898, Jane was left with 11 children to raise. The store and a boarding house behind it managed to sustain them. Once the sole emporium in the village, today Mouat's is surrounded by restaurants, boutiques and art galleries, all very prettily built around Grace Point Square and its dockside boardwalk. The Saturday Market in Centennial Park draws crowds of shoppers onto the island.

From the bustle of Ganges, head south on the Fulford-Ganges Road for about two kilometres, then turn right on Cranberry Road. This leads gently up into the hills, passing pioneer Foxglove Farm, to meet Mount Maxwell Road for a steep nine-kilometre climb almost to the summit of Mount Maxwell Provincial Park's Baynes Peak, one of the highest points on the island. The road winds first though stands of Garry oak, then into evergreen woodlands. The last part of the road is unpaved and could be rough and wet, but continue on: a short walk from the parking lot leads to an outstanding view from the sandstone clifftop down to the stitched green meadows of the Fulford Valley, east across a labyrinth of islands to the mainland and west to the mountains of Vancouver Island. One can watch hawks and eagles soaring far below and count the tiny painted ships upon the painted ocean of Burgoyne Bay. Sunsets here are magnificent, and the woodlands engender a deep sense of wilderness. The mountain reserve is home to black bear, deer, turkey vultures and peregrine falcons, an amazing diversity for such a small and populated island. The crowds in Ganges Village seem far, far away.

Back on the Fulford-Ganges Road, continue south through farmlands and vineyards under the shadow of Mount Maxwell to Burgoyne Bay Road, which goes west past a derelict farmhouse and huge barn down to a pebble beach, ringed with eelgrass beds and marshy wetlands. The deep sheltered bay, with its public wharf, provides good moorage for sailboats. With its clam beds and salmon spawning grounds, the bay was a gathering place for coastal First Nations who knew it as Hwaaqwum, or "place of mergansers." Archeologists have uncovered a dozen sites here—shell middens, burials and fish weirs—from some 3,000 years of occupation. Now a provincial park, Burgoyne Bay and its farmlands adjoin Mount Maxwell in the north and Mount Sullivan in the south to create one huge protected area, part of the Gulf Islands National Park Reserve.

From the Burgoyne Bay intersection, the main route swings east and meanders down to Fulford Harbour. Along the way, look for some of the historic buildings that survive here, such as 1887 Burgoyne United Church behind its neat picket fence, St. Mary's church, built in 1894, and several pioneer farmhouses.

At the head of Fulford Harbour, Isabella Point Road curves past Drummond Park, where lawns shaded with huge old maples slope down to a beach, a good place to watch the ferry from Swartz Bay sailing into dock across the inlet. A large boulder carved with a petroglyph of a seal was found underwater and moved near the playground here. Past the park, Musgrave Road angles up the slopes of Mount Tuam, a peak spiritually significant for local First Nations. Along here are the fields of the Sacred Mountain Lavender farm, at their best in July. Musgrave Road, steep and gravelled, wriggles between Hope Hill and Mount Bruce to isolated Musgrave Landing, where Edward Musgrave once ran a prosperous sheep farm that is now a private estate. Isabella Point Road continues south past the Ruby Alton Nature Reserve. In the gardens of Ruby's 1930s house is a King William pear tree that dates from 1890.

Fulford Village, at the head of the inlet, still has its comfortable old inn that looks across the harbour to the village centre on Morningside Road, the ferry dock and fishboats in the marina. St. Paul's Church nearby was constructed in 1880 by Catholic missionary Father Donckele, assistant to Father Peter Rondeault, who built the Butter Church at Cowichan (see Chapter 7), and the two stone churches look very similar. The sandstone blocks for St. Paul's were quarried from Comiaken Hill, near Cowichan Bay and ferried across by dug-out canoe, then hauled to

Ruckle Provincial Park was deeded to the province by the pioneer Ruckle family, which still farms here on land they originally settled in 1872. Their old orchards still bloom in the spring.

128

the site by ox-drawn stoneboat. When the church in Cowichan was abandoned, its bell, door and a stained glass window were put to good use here. Local Hawaiians (known as Kanakas), brought to B.C. to work for the Hudson's Bay Company, helped to build the church. When their contracts were finished, many chose to stay in Canada, and the company gave them Portland Island, just offshore. (The uninhabited island is now Princess Margaret Marine Park.) Several Kanakas settled on Salt Spring and are buried in St Paul's churchyard.

Take Beaver Point Road from Fulford Village around Weston Lake and keep on to Beaver Point, named for the famous HBC steamship. Beaver Point School, which opened in 1885 and is the second oldest in B.C., sits near the intersection with Bridgeman Road. It's now a daycare centre. Drive on to Ruckle Provincial Park, the largest park in the Gulf Islands, covering nearly 500 hectares of land at the island's southeastern edge. The area was settled by Henry and Anna Ruckle, who arrived on Salt Spring in 1872 with a flock of sheep, built a homestead and planted an apple orchard. A hundred years later, the family sold the land for a park but stayed on to farm the property, making it the oldest continuously worked farm on the island. Park headquarters are in the "potato house," built in 1938 by William Ruckle for his bride-to-be. When the wedding was cancelled, the house was abandoned and used for potato storage. Only a part of the Ruckle land was cleared. Trails lead through woodlands and along seven kilometres of coastline, where grassy headlands provide views out to Swanson Channel and Portland Island.

Outside the park, a cross-hatch of small lanes leads to some interesting artisans typical of the back-to-the-land philosophy of the island. Notable along Forest Ridge Road are a one-woman bakery where bread is cooked in a wood-fired oven, and an organic orchard/farm that

A ferry noses into Fulford Harbour. Salt Spring has three ferry terminals, with service from the mainland, Swartz Bay and Buckley Bay.

130

grows 200 different kinds of apples, garlic, roses and free-range chickens. Just before the junction with Stewart Road, the return route north, turn up Reynolds Road to visit the Salt Spring Island Cheese Company, whose handmade goat's and sheep's milk cheeses, often decorated with edible garden flowers, have become very popular.

Continue north along Stewart Road, then swing right onto Beddis Road. At the road's south end, the white sand and shells of Beddis Beach make it a popular swimming destination. North on Beddis, one of the island's heritage roads, are more farm-gate operations, including another fine cheese maker and another apple farm. Beddis leads back onto Fulford-Ganges Road, the island's "highway."

For a different return route to the ferry, once you reach Ganges, turn left (west) down Rainbow

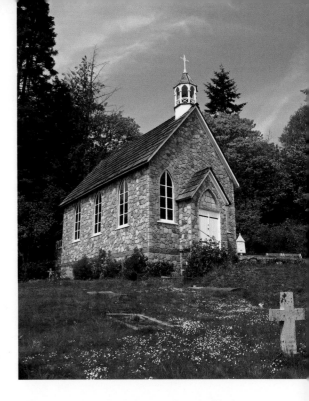

The stone church of St. Paul at Fulford may seem familiar: it was built in 1888 by the same people, and with the same stone, as the Butter Church near Duncan.

Road. Pioneer Estalon Bittancourt's house, which dates from 1880, has been moved onto the Farmers Institute grounds on Rainbow Road and is now the Ganges Museum. The house has been restored and furnished in period style, and is open to the public by appointment. Turn right on Canal Road, which bridges the inlet at the head of Booth Bay and leads back into Vesuvius, a wonderful place to watch the sunset.

To visit some of the artists' studios on Salt Spring, pick up a detailed Studio Tour road map, which shows the locations and information on all the participating artists and craftsmen. Another map, Salt Spring Island Greenwise, documents all the farms and food producers. Copies are widely available at Visitor Centres on Vancouver Island or in Ganges. ❖

As soon as one leaves the coastal plain that rims the southern and eastern shores of Vancouver Island, the fields and farms surrender to the forest. Dropped like a cloak over the steep mountains and valleys, these forests are still beautiful, although they have been often brutally logged and are now into their second and third growths. Richly green, clumped with moss and tangled with ferns and flowers, their quiet shadows and streams provide a very different country road experience. For the most part, the roads through the forest are or were logging roads, cut through the valleys as expeditiously as possible to get the logs to market. Most of them are unpaved, but without them, the forest would be impenetrable.

This east-west route starts at Duncan on the east coast of Vancouver Island, follows the Cowichan River to Cowichan Lake and dives into the heart of logging country, through the forests to Bamfield on the west coast. Cowichan Lake is encircled by an easy-to-drive 80-kilometre loop road, and this could very well be enough for those who don't relish the thought of rough, isolated logging-road travel. But driving the rest of the way west, another 80 kilometres into the Nitinat Valley and across to Bamfield, will provide a deeper forest experience and will bring you to one of the most charming and unusual fishing villages along the coast.

Highway 18 is the most direct route from Duncan to Lake Cowichan, but there is a slower and prettier road. It closely follows the north bank of the Cowichan River and gives access to the Cowichan River Footpath, cut through the forest by the Cowichan Fish and Game Association in the 1960s and now part of the Trans-Canada Trail. The Cowichan is a famous fishing stream, renowned for its brown trout.

Duncan is a town that drew attention by commissioning more than 80 totem poles to decorate city streets. In the summer, free, guided walking tours to 37 of the downtown poles are

The lovely Cowichan River, famous for its feisty brown trout, is accessible via Riverbottom Road and the Trans-Canada Trail all the way from Duncan to Lake Cowichan.

132

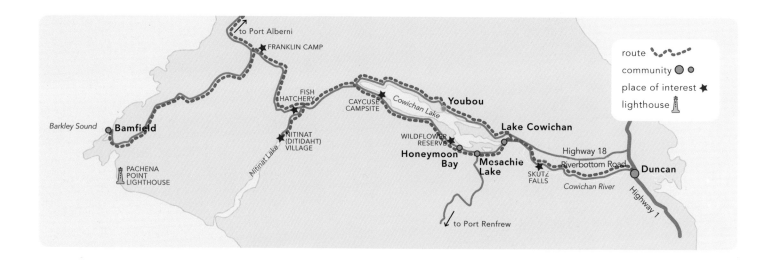

accompanied by vivid descriptions and by some of the local myths. The tours begin from the heritage 1887 Esquimalt & Nanaimo station, now a museum. Painted yellow footprints along city sidewalks also direct walkers to the totems. Beside the Cowichan River on the town outskirts is the Quw'utsun' Cultural and Conference Centre, where Coast Salish arts and crafts, totems, and dance and potlatch regalia, are all splendidly displayed. Here, too, are carvers, chiselling away at poles and masks, and knitters busily working with hand-spun raw wool to create the traditional Cowichan sweaters, which are sold around the world.

Before European settlement, the First Nations women were already weavers, using hair from wild mountain goats spun together with wool from small domestic dogs (a species now extinct), which they sheared with mussel-shell knives. Settlers introduced domestic sheep in the 1850s, and when the Sisters of St. Ann arrived in 1864 to start a school, they brought with them knitting needles and taught local girls to knit socks and mittens from sheep's wool. Cowichan women were quick to adopt the new technique (and the new fibre) and copied knit-and-purl patterns from the sweaters of Scottish sailors. In 1885 Jeremina Colvin, wife of a sheep farmer at Cowichan Station, began knitting the multicoloured Fair Isle designs she remembered from her childhood in the Shetland Islands, and she taught the technique to women on the Koksilah reserve. Soon they were knitting thick, homespun wool sweaters, using the different natural colours of the fleece to reproduce traditional tribal designs. Knit mostly in the round, the sweaters are both warm and rain-resistant and are always in demand.

From downtown Duncan, take Government Street north to Gibbins Road. Five kilometres along this pleasantly wooded suburban route, turn left along Barnjum Road, an unpaved two-kilometre connector to Riverbottom Road. Turn left to drive parallel to the Cowichan River, at first fairly high above it—the water sparkles enticingly through the forest fringe. Most of the

Though the original forests around Cowichan Lake were harvested a long time ago, the second- and third-growth woods are lovely, jungled with ferns and interspersed with deciduous trees.

land is within Cowichan River Provincial Park, but the forest is not pristine. It has all been logged, and, though replanted in the 1980s and '90s, it will be years before the young trees reach full growth. Stop at the Marie Canyon picnic area for a close-up river view; at a pull-off just beyond, a clifftop trail provides a wonderful overlook. In Marie Canyon (Mile 66 Trestle) Day Use Area, a footpath leads down to one of the old railway trestles that crossed the river, now the track for the Trans-Canada Trail.

Riverbottom Road climbs and twists and finally arrives right by the river at Skutz Falls, a series of chattering rapids where fish ladders were built in 1955 to help salmon migrate upstream. The recreation area, with its picnic tables, is popular with kayakers. Beyond the falls, the road climbs back toward Highway 18. Just before the highway, turn left on Old Cowichan Lake Road and follow this quieter route to the town of Lake Cowichan. Behind the Visitor Centre, the town's museum is housed in the former Kaatza Station of an E & N Railway spur line that was established in 1911 to bring logs from lakeside camps to the coast for shipment.

One of the old engines lies alongside the museum. Kaatza is the Lake Cowichan First Nation's name for Cowichan Lake: it simply means Big Lake, and it is a big lake—at 30 kilometres long, it is one of the largest on Vancouver Island. Popularized by British royalty (it was a favourite of King Edward VIII), the lake has been renowned for fishing since the Lake Cowichan tribe camped here. Commercial logging started early. The huge Douglas firs that grew around the lake were easily accessed from the water and were hauled away in log booms. A road was cut

from the coast to the end of the lake in 1885 and was extended in increments along the shoreline to logging camps, mill sites and company towns. The fast-growing forest around the lake has covered the scars of a century of scalping, and much of it today looks thick and green and lovely, at least from the road.

Unless you are heading straight to Bamfield, take South Shore Road for a clockwise circuit of the lake. This road cuts inland on its way to the small settlement of Mesachie Lake, a former mill town built by Hillcrest Lumber in the 1940s on the shore of a small lake of the same name. The neat rows of company houses remain, and so do the trees: more than 200 fruit, ornamental and shade trees were imported by the company and planted here. Now protected as heritage trees, they fringe the road through town. On a peninsula jutting into the lake nearby is Cowichan Lake Forest Research Station, founded in 1929 for the study of tree genetics, disease control and optimum growth. Thousands of saplings from seeds, cuttings and grafts are grown here for study and replanting. For the first seven years before the road finally came through, research station supplies and workers were shuttled in and out by boat, and the several hundred residents were accommodated in bunkhouses. The bunkhouses and the log cookhouse, the last of its kind in the area, are still in use as a conference centre. Public tours of the operations are given in summer months.

Recently, the paving of a logging road route south on Hillcrest and Harris Creek mainlines has provided comfortable access from Mesachie Lake to Port Renfrew on the west coast. (Paved or not, it is still a forestry road; watch for loaded logging trucks.) The road passes two notable forest giants, the Harris Creek Spruce and the San Juan Sitka Spruce.

An early-morning boater enjoys the morning mists on Cowichan Lake as he approaches Caycuse Campsite.

136

Honeymoon Bay, a couple of kilometres farther west, was first settled in 1887 by Henry March, who harnessed oxen and horses to help clear his land. Taking his hay and other produce to market entailed a three-day trip—the first part by raft to the end of the lake, then by ox-drawn wagon along rough trails to Duncan. His original log farmhouse and enormous barn still remain, neglected and shrouded in greenery across from March Meadows Golf Club, which is built on the former farm's hay-fields. The old orchard of gnarled apple, pear and plum trees provides a favourite munching place for black bears. March chose his site wisely: the southern arm of the lake has the warmest water in Canada, enjoying summer temperatures of up to 24°C. Test the waters at Lily Beach Park. Today's community, another former mill town, grew up beside the March farm. The lines of small company homes divided by narrow lanes stretch away from the lake.

The road near Skutz Falls is coloured with fall maples. Skutz Falls has fish ladders to aid with migration.

The stately trillium is just one of the wildflowers protected in the Honeymoon Bay Ecological Reserve.

Just west of town, turn right on Walton Road to visit Gordon Bay Provincial Park, with its sandy beach and groves of tall second-growth Douglas fir. Beyond the golf course on South Shore Road is Honeymoon Bay Ecological Reserve, six hectares set aside mostly because of the spring wildflower displays. Among the two dozen different varieties, one flower in particular brings botanists in from afar: a rare pink variety of the delicate erythronium, or fawn lily, which grows here in abundance in April and May. The reserve is not well signed; watch for a small parking area at the trailhead.

From Honeymoon Bay, the road west turns to gravel and edges closer to the lake, providing ethereal views across the water to the mountains along the north shore. On misty fall days, when dappled sunlight edges the lush greens of ferns and mosses, the woods are wonderful indeed. About 10 kilometres along is Caycuse Campsite, one of the loveliest along the shore. Here, the bigleaf maple trees are themselves big—old-growth giants, furred with thick bumpy moss. In fall, their leaves light up like golden flags. Farther along is the site of Caycuse logging camp, known as Camp 6, yet another of the old company towns. There's not much left of this townsite, apart from the office and the old recreation centre, and it is all private property.

At the intersection with Caycuse Main logging road, South Shore Road (turn right here) becomes a private forest road, though it is accessible to the public; it is steep and rough. A right turn beyond popular Heather Campsite at the head of the lake leads to Youbou Road for completion of the circle route back to Lake Cowichan along the lake's northern shore. The road surface on Youbou Road is good, making for a pleasant drive, much of it either directly along the lake or high enough above the trees to allow for beautiful views. The mountain shoreline is steeper here,

A short hike from Bamfield leads to long Brady's Beach, with its interesting sea stacks. Across Trevor Channel lie the islands of the Deer Group.

and the creeks roar down. Shaw Creek, with its tangled meadows, and McKay Creek provide good trout fishing where they enter the lake. Just west of Cottonwood Creek is Youbou, once the largest company mill town on the lake, named for Mr. Yount and Mr. Bouten, respectively manager and president of the company. The mill, like others here, is closed and the land up for development, but an interesting discovery gives a glimpse into the townsite's history.

A tombstone etched with Chinese calligraphy for the name Zheng Weijing and a date of 1925 is a relic of a small lumber operation on Cottonwood Creek, where a settlement known as Yap Alley housed immigrants of several nationalities. The Chinese bunkhouse and the graveyard were once considered for heritage status, but the bunkhouse burned and the plan was scrapped. The old company town along the lake edge merges easily today with modern subdivisions, and basic services are still provided here in the second-largest settlement on the lake. North Shore Road runs along the lake from Youbou to finish the circuit back at Lake Cowichan.

Explorers who choose to push all the way to the west coast usually start by following the road along Cowichan Lake's north shore, and this route is the easiest to follow. Paving ends beyond Youbou, but the industrial road is fairly smooth until it reaches the head of the lake. Beyond here, expect dust or mud and large logging trucks, so drive carefully with headlights on and be on the alert for signposts. At the lakehead, drive straight through a prominent inter-section, passing Kissinger Lake Campsite, and turn left on the road signposted to Nitinat (or Ditidaht), then right, following the signs. Past the Ditidaht Forest Products mill site, a left turn leads to Nitinat Lake and the giant old trees of the Carmanah Valley, which were saved from logging by active citizen protests.

The Ditidaht First Nation village (seven kilometres from the junction) seems like an oasis of civilization in the forested mountains. Its combined general store, motel and restaurant provides for all tourist needs, even gasoline, and it is a fountain of information on fishing, windsurfing, camping and general directions. The village is a point of departure for the wilderness hiking routes in the Carmanah and along the West Coast Trail: the narrows at the end of the saltwater lake is the trail's halfway point, and hikers can register at the store and take a water taxi to start their journey. Nitinat "lake," really a very long, narrow and almost landlocked inlet of the sea, has become famous for windsurfing, ranking in the top 10 destinations in the world. In summer, local campsites are crowded with surfers on the international circuit.

If you drive to the village, you will follow the Nitinat River to the lakehead, where Nitinat River Hatchery, Canada's largest, rears thousands of chum, chinook, coho and steelhead, some in the net pens visible on the right. The view of the lake alone is well worth the side trip. To get to Bamfield, keep going straight at the Nitinat intersection, cross the river bridge (to visit the hatchery, turn left immediately after the bridge) and join a short stretch of paved road to Franklin Camp. Started in the 1930s, the camp was once home to the world's largest logging operation, with accommodation for 455 families and 40 bunkhouses for 320 single men. The mill here was the first in North America to use power saws (1936) and the first to require its workers to use hard hats (1942). Turn left before the camp onto Bamfield Road, and stay on it the rest of the way.

Bamfield, the end (or the beginning) of the West Coast Trail from Port Renfrew, is rapidly changing its persona. A fishing village straddling a narrow inlet, it has been only fairly recently accessible by road, allowing hikers to get in and out very easily (there is even a local bus service from

Half of the village of Bamfield lies across a narrow inlet and can be reached only by boat or water taxi. A sturdy boardwalk provides access.

Port Alberni). The village has become quite the tourist destination; part of its charm lies is that only half of it is accessible by car. The rest lies across the inlet and is reached only by boat. A water-taxi service crosses to the west side, which is pretty and—at least in summer—very tourist friendly.

A sturdy shoreline boardwalk connects all the buildings, including some homes, a few shops, the general store, the post office, tourist accommodation and services (including an interesting cat garden, where strays are housed and fed in miniature landmark replicas, such as the Cape Beale Lighthouse). Behind the general store, Kings Road leads to Brady's Beach, with its picturesque sea stacks and great sunsets. Three times a week, the MV *Frances Barkley*, a working freighter, arrives at the government dock beside the Coast Guard station, bringing hikers, kayakers and day trippers down from Port Alberni after uploading supplies to isolated settlements along the way (see Chapter 14).

Bamfield's east side is the terminal point for both the logging road and the West Coast Trail from Port Renfrew. It was also the terminus for the first trans-Pacific telegraph cable, laid in 1902 and kept in service for more than 50 years until the line was extended to Port Alberni. The telegraph building was then put to use as a marine station and now supports the research work of five Canadian universities. High on the hillside, it's the biggest building in Bamfield. The east side of the inlet houses the church, school, community hall and commercial services, including some great B & Bs. But even the east side is not totally road-accessible. Drive to the head of a small inlet (east of the east side of Bamfield Inlet) to a pretty cove called Port Desire and look from the dock at all the little houses across the water that can only be reached by boat.

The 1907 Pachena Point Lighthouse is less than 10 kilometres southeast along the first part of the West Coast Trail; one can drive part of the way there, to wide Pachena Bay. The First Nation

141

village of Anacla has a riverside park here, complete with totems and a beachside forest campsite. Also drive down the sign-posted road to the West Coast Trailhead in Pacific Rim National Park. The access road winds carefully around some huge old-growth trees, and from the meadow in front of the registration building, a short trail leads out to the beach.

From Bamfield, a return loop north can be driven on the "main" road along Alberni Inlet to Port Alberni (40 kilometres). This road, though still unpaved for most of the way, is well used by the general public as well as by logging trucks and fishermen. For this route, return the way you came toward Franklin Camp, but turn left, following signs to Port Alberni. Paved road starts again near China Creek, a popular marina and campsite, usually full of RVs. Port Alberni is on Highway 4, one of the few cross-Island routes linking the Strait of Georgia to the west coast. ❧

Inhabitants of Port Desire must rely on boats to reach the "civilized" part of Bamfield for supplies and services. A small rowboat tied up at the mainland dock awaits its owner for the journey home.

12   TWO ISLAND SOLITUDES

Why do small islands conjure feelings of magic and mystery? Does their isolation breed
enchantment? Does the alien world of water that surrounds them add to their alchemy? In the
sheltered waters of Queen Charlotte Sound just offshore from the town of Port McNeill are two
islands, one small, one very small, each with a very different persona. One is redolent with First
Nations history, old and new; the other echoes with the dashed dreams of immigrant Utopia.
Both are wonderful places to experience that island sense of strange.

B.C. Ferries, the islands' lifeline, connects Port McNeill with Alert Bay on Cormorant Island
and Sointula on Malcolm Island. Tickets are sold on a return basis. The zigzag schedule is weird
and wonderful, at least to outsiders. Berthed at Alert Bay, the ferry makes six return runs daily
to Port McNeill and five from Port McNeill to Sointula. Only the last ferry from Alert Bay
stops at Sointula en route; otherwise, to get from Sointula to Alert Bay and vice versa, passengers must first return to Port McNeill, disembark and get on again. It sounds more complicated
than it is—and somehow this enhances the charm of these little islands. Just make sure you
have the ferry schedule in hand, and tell the attendant your destination. You might be handed a
"turn-around pass." The crossings are short and very pleasant as they manoeuvre through the
maritime traffic in Broughton Strait and around tiny Haddington Island, where the andesite
limestone destined for the B.C. Legislative Buildings in Victoria was quarried.

Cormorant Island was named in 1846 for a British naval vessel and its deep bay for another
British ship, the HMS *Alert*. A sliver of sand and gravel washed up by glaciers, the island is
small, barely eight kilometres long, with low, forested hills behind the bay. It is marginally drier
than most of the north coast, since it is in the rain shadow of Vancouver's Island's mountains. It
sits in waters once teeming with killer whales, porpoises, dolphins, seals and sea lions, and fish

*Port McNeill is the
home port for BC
Ferries trips to Alert
Bay and Sointula.
It is also home
to a large fishing
fleet, whose boat
reflections fill the
harbour waters
with a kaleidoscope
of colour.*

144

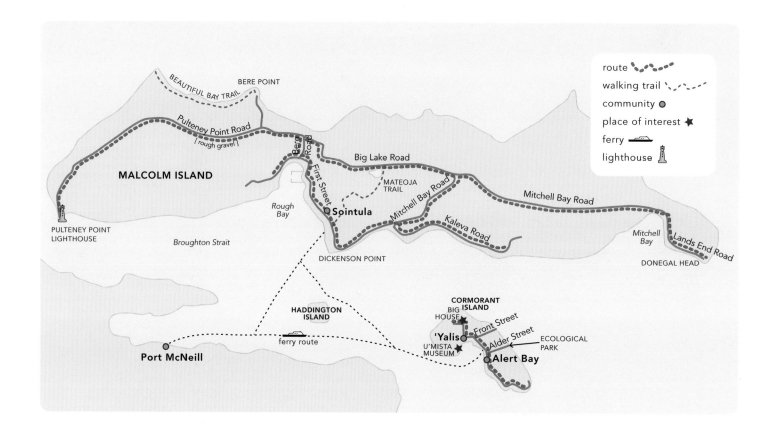

of many kinds. The Kwakiutl (Kwakwaka'wakw) First Nation traditionally visited the island for summer food gathering and for a burial ground, but it was almost deserted when the first Europeans arrived. In 1870, Alden Huson, whose name appears often in local history, leased the whole island for 21 years, paying the crown colony $40 a year. With his partner, Stephen Spencer, he started a small factory for salt-curing herring and salmon for shipment to Victoria, and he employed people of the 'Namgis First Nation, who canoed to work from their village at the mouth of the Nimpkish River across the strait. Eight years later, Huson's business had grown and he needed workers closer to hand. To encourage settlement close to the factory, he persuaded the Anglican missionary at nearby Fort Rupert to come to Alert Bay and build a church and a school. 'Namgis tribal members followed and established the traditional village, 'Yalis, around the mission nucleus. In 1881, Huson and partners opened a salmon cannery, the first between the Fraser River and the Skeena. Other immigrants arrived, and Alert Bay expanded into a lively fishing village. When the Dominion Wireless service was established here in 1912, the village boomed.

Huson's lease on the whole island eventually lapsed, and later treaties allotted most of the western section to the 'Namgis, effectively splitting the island into First Nations' and non-Native

land. The two come together at the ferry dock where an ornate welcome archway carved by Chief Doug Cranmer represents Sisiutl, the two-headed sea serpent, an appropriate choice. Turn right on Fir Street for Alert Bay village, left on Front Street for 'Yalis. More than two-thirds of the population of Cormorant Island are of First Nations heritage, and 'Yalis is home to the province's largest Aboriginal fishing fleet.

Alert Bay's deep harbour is fronted by wharves and old fish-packing plants, net lofts and assorted sheds, many of them built over tidewater. One of the largest, a huge net loft sprawled out into the bay on pilings, was built in 1949 by the Anglo-British Columbia Packing Company and is still in use by the 'Namgis. A smart new wooden boardwalk starts at the ferry dock and continues all the way west around the bay past historic Christ Church, with its spiky gingerbread trim and neat white picket fence. The church opened on Christmas Day, 1892. Services are held here in both English and Kwakwala, and prayer books and hymnals are also bilingual. The adjacent St. George's Chapel, built in 1925, houses the former St. Michael's Residential School bible, dating to 1850.

Around the scoop of the bay, west of the church, the road ends near the U'Mista Cultural Centre and museum, a stunning replica of a former Big House from 1873. In an effort to indoctrinate First Nations into European ways, traditional celebrations, including potlatches, were forbidden for many years. Tribal artifacts were seized by the government, part of a cultural prohibition that was eventually reversed, but not

The U'mista Cultural Centre and Museum at 'Yalis houses a huge collection of old 'Namgis potlatch regalia.

before the priceless possessions had been dispersed, some to museums around the world. But there has been a welcome change of heart: many of the confiscated artifacts, symbols of tribal heritage and prestige, have been returned and with them, a resurgence of cultural pride ensures that the language, traditions and history of the 'Namgis will continue. The reclaimed artifacts are magnificently displayed in the U'mista museum, a large wooden building beside the beach, guarded by two totems looking out to sea. The house's front design in black and white depicts a thunderbird and a whale. (The name U'Mista is fitting: it means something like "those who have returned," a term originally applied to people captured in battle, and usually enslaved, who somehow made their way home again.)

Near the Cultural Centre, the sombre hulk of St. Michael's brick residential school, with its memories of an unhappy era, is derelict and may soon be torn down. Look for some carved and decorated cedar canoes stored outside and carvers at work in the basement. It's a short walk from the museum through the village to the present-day Big House and the second-tallest pole in B.C., carved with figures from several local family clans and topped by a giant Sun Man. It is so tall (173 feet) that it can be seen from far out at sea. On the hillside behind, the large new cemetery contains a wealth of memorial poles as well as traditional Christian grave markers. The artistry here is amazing.

The 'Namgis Big House, with its painted facade and eagle-topped totem, sits beside the ball field. In summer months, the huge building is open to the public for performances by the T'sasala Dance Group. While the events are geared primarily for tourists, they are splendidly done: the audience becomes immersed in the ancient rituals and legends as costumed dancers

spin and weave around the fire to the insistent beat of the drums. Sparks rise like fireflies, the smoke wreathes and rises and spills around the dancers, and the whole tableau becomes blurred and hazy as history itself. It is as if the ghosts of the past are dancing here. The performances inside this imposing traditional structure with its totems, potlatch bowls and cedar-tree drum are unforgettable.

A right turn off the ferry dock leads along Fir Street to the heart of the non-Native part of the village, still anchored by the 1920 waterfront Nimpkish Hotel, first built on reserve lands but towed to its present location soon afterward so that it could include a beer parlour. A brick-paved Victorian promenade is edged along the shoreline by an ornamental balustrade for an oh-so-British effect. The Customs House is now a B & B, the Visitor Centre/museum is in the old firehall, and what was once the combined police station, jail and courthouse is now a doctor's office. Alert Bay Shipyards Ltd., dating from 1908, was started by a son of pioneer Alden Huson.

On the landward side of Fir Street, beside the now-derelict nurses' residence (the nearby St. George's Mission hospital burned down in 1923), is the old 'Namgis burial ground, its forest of mortuary poles bearing family crests: frog, grizzly bear, thunderbird, eagle, raven and halibut. Among them are the oldest poles in B.C. still on their original site, some dating to the 1870s. Closest to the road is a stout uncarved pole topped by a Haida mortuary transformation panel which depicts Raven. This was carved in memory of the 300 Haida families, infected with smallpox, who were sent into quarantine at Bones Bay in Kwakwaka'wakw lands in 1862, never to return home. When the road east from the town centre was rebuilt, it cut through part of this

historic cemetery. The people buried under what is now blacktop were honoured in 1995 by the erection of two poles: the Giant Halibut Totem, and Thunderbird, Man Holding a Copper. (Native coppers, hand-beaten into shield-like objects, were a sign of wealth and prestige.) Each pole has a story to tell, a family to remember. The graveyard is sacred and out of bounds for tourists, but it is easily viewed from the surrounding streets.

Head up Alder Street to Alert Bay Ecological Park, where boardwalk trails lead through a swamp made eerie by the presence of dead grey snags draped in moss. Known locally as Gator Gardens and frequented by eagles, ravens and other wildlife, the reserve marshes were formed when a small creek was dammed to provide fresh water for the first salmon cannery.

At about 24 kilometres long, Malcolm Island is three times the size of Cormorant, though only 3 kilometres wide. As the ferry sidles up to the wharf, the first sign to greet the traveller announces the island's heritage. The big yellow building is the Sointula Cooperative Store, B.C.'s oldest, and has been the commercial and social centre of this fishing village since 1909.

Sointula is Finnish for "Place of Harmony" and this was the dream of the Kalevan Kansa Colonization Company, a group of Finnish settlers who arrived here in 1901 in search of their vision of Utopia. The socialistic commune was granted ownership of the whole island and set about clearing land for crops and building homes, a foundry, brickyard, sawmill and blacksmith's shop. Despite hard work, the colony suffered serious setbacks. In 1903 their large communal hall burned, killing 11 people and destroying valuable supplies and records. The following year, one of their leaders left, taking with him a group of disillusioned settlers, and in 1905 the company itself went bankrupt. Most colony members moved away, and the island lands, except for the small plots

LEFT *Stony beaches along Kaleva Road look southeast across Broughton Channel to Cormorant Island and the mountains of Vancouver Island. A spring rainstorm adds drama.*

of those who stayed behind, reverted back to the Crown. Yet, a hundred years later, the Finnish influence is still deep on the island, as a quick look through a telephone directory will show, and traces of the old fishing village, with its plank houses and separate saunas, survive here.

There are two driving routes on the island: one around the southern shore on 1st Street and Kaleva Road, and another that bisects the wooded heart of the island, from Pulteney Point in the west to Mitchell Bay in the east. Both are dead-end roads. Sointula village, an interesting cross-hatch of streets terraced back from the waterfront, clusters north of the ferry dock. Drive east (right from the ferry) around Dickenson Point to the pioneer cemetery at Kaleva Point and on along the stony beachfront, with its small farms and homesteads carved out of the woods behind. Along Kaleva Road look for the Wirkki house and a weather-beaten, squint-eyed shed set back behind a rope fence decorated with fishing floats—an appropriate touch, since Victor Wirkki was a fisherman. This house is one of the last authentic Finnish settlers' cottages, and it is still basically unaltered. Kaleva Road faces out across Cormorant Channel to views of mountains and islands. It's a wild and somehow lonely view, and the stony beach makes for an excellent stroll.

Retrace your route through the village (do visit the large Co-op Store) and head west along the 1st Street waterfront to see the museum, a working forge and the grand Finnish Organization Hall, and then on to the fishing harbour in the mouth of Rough Bay. All along the way, there's a wealth of old wharves, net lofts and boat sheds lining the beach, many of them on pilings.

By Rough Bay harbour, head north on Bere Road to the second driving route. Take Big Lake Road east through the woods onto Mitchell Bay Road. Mitchell Bay itself is a small community

OPPOSITE *A wind whips up waves by the Sointula ferry dock. In the distance is the town of Port McNeill.*

with a Government Wharf and a stony, grass-edged beach. The road continues on to Donegal Head and Lands End Road, where one of the island's B & Bs is an oxen farm with a blacksmith forge (free lessons at the anvil for its guests). The blacksmith here regularly demonstrates his skills at the museum in town.

Return to the Bere Road intersection and head west, past the signs to Bere Point Regional Park and Beautiful Bay Trail, onto Pulteney Point Road, which leads 11 kilometres across the island to one of the few staffed lighthouses in B.C. This road is narrow, wooded, hilly and unpaved; expect dust and many deer. Park at the lighthouse gates and find the narrow trail that leads down through the woods to an extensive pebble beach. Left around the point will bring a fine view of the lighthouse and its cluster of red-roofed buildings. It's an easy 15-minute walk, but remember to mark where the trail hits the beach. On the return, the trail is sometimes difficult to find, particularly

A short walk along a beautiful pebble beach leads to Pulteney Point Lighthouse at the southwestern tip of Malcolm Island. This is a great place to watch the sunset.

at dusk. The sunsets here are worth waiting for. The lighthouse is operated by the Coast Guard, and only the grounds are open to the public.

Hikers can check at the Sointula Resource Centre on 1st Street for a map of the island and its two main hiking trails. One, an interesting three-kilometre stretch known as the Mateoja Heritage Trail, leads through woodlands and marshes to the pioneer farmlands of the Mateoja family and on to the local swimming hole at Big Lake. It is well signed. The five-kilometre Beautiful Bay Trail along the north coast cliffs to Malcolm Point makes a great day walk. Highlights include several lookouts, a dramatic canyon, eagles' nests and a giant Sitka spruce. Look also for whales, seals and sea lions. The return trip can be made along the beach, if the tide cooperates. ✣

Two powerful totems stand in front of the now-derelict brick residential school at 'Yalis on Cormorant Island. Visitors can watch traditional dances in the Big House, enjoy a salmon barbecue or take a journey in a cedar dugout canoe.

13

DISCOVERY ISLANDS

Quadra is the largest of a maze of islands that sit like corks in the northern bottleneck of the Strait of Georgia known as Discovery Passage. These, the Discovery Islands, almost block the main shipping route along the Inside Passage. The only navigable channel threads between Vancouver Island and Quadra's western shore, making the island easily accessible by ferry from Campbell River, a 10-minute cruise that seems to lead from one world to another. Quadra's whole population is less than a tenth that of Campbell River's, and its three little villages have a decidedly laid-back and unsophisticated air. Here you will find no shopping malls, no big-box stores, no four-lane highways—none of the conveniences of the big city so close to Quadra that, from some spots, you can see its street lights at night.

Early settlement focussed in the south, where most of the population lives today and where most visitors choose to stay. The south is also a First Nations stronghold. On the island's southern tip, the 600-metre-high bluffs at Cape Mudge guard the entrance to the only navigable channel north, one that is still fraught with dangerous rocks and riptides. Traditionally, Cape Mudge was the boundary—always in dispute—between the Coast Salish of the south and the warrior tribes of the Kwakiutl (now Kwakwaka'wakw), who lived in the north. Here the two cultures clashed, often and sometimes catastrophically. The large Coast Salish village on the clifftop recorded by botanist Archibald Menzies in 1792 had vanished 60 years later, replaced by a new Kwakwaka'wakw village on the shore below. Today, old animosities have been assuaged, and the island today offers a comfortable juxtaposition of First Nations and European history—and enough little roads to accommodate a day's exploration of both cultures. Set aside another day to explore the delights of Cortes Island, attached to Quadra by ferry from Heriot Bay. Its remoteness adds to its country charms.

North Quadra Island is still deeply forested, and its residents tuck themselves away in tranquil places such as this.

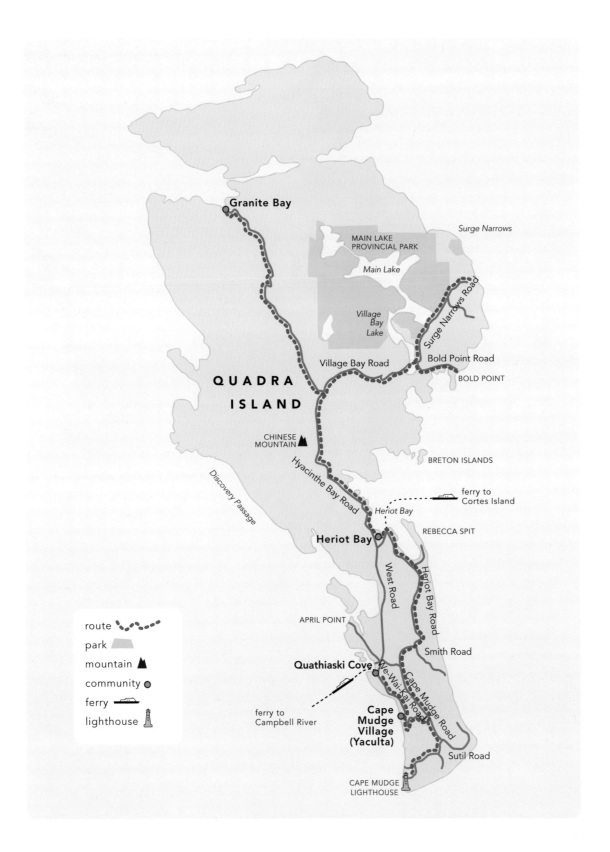

Granite Bay

Surge Narrows

MAIN LAKE
PROVINCIAL PARK

Main Lake

Village
Bay
Lake

QUADRA
ISLAND

Village Bay Road

Surge Narrows Road

Bold Point Road

BOLD POINT

CHINESE
MOUNTAIN

Discovery Passage

Hyacinthe Bay Road

BRETON ISLANDS

ferry to
Cortes Island

Heriot Bay

Heriot Bay

REBECCA SPIT

West Road

Heriot Bay Road

APRIL POINT

Smith Road

route
park
mountain
community
ferry
lighthouse

Quathiaski Cove

We-Wai-Kai Road

Cape Mudge Road

ferry to
Campbell River

Cape
Mudge
Village
(Yaculta)

Sutil Road

CAPE MUDGE
LIGHTHOUSE

How did Quadra get it name? During sovereignty negotiations in 1792 at Nootka between the British and the Spanish, Captain Vancouver became close friends with his counterpart, Don Juan Francisco de la Bodega y Quadra and gave both their names, Quadra and Vancouver, to what later became simply Vancouver Island. To compensate Quadra for this loss, though well after his death, this little piece of B.C. was named after him.

The ferry from Campbell River docks at Quathiaski Cove, a descriptive Salish word meaning "a mouth with a bite of something in it," the "something" being fat little Grouse Island, just offshore. It was in this cove on the protected inner thigh of the island that Vancouver's sailing ships, the *Discovery* and the *Chatham*, first anchored after rounding Cape Mudge (named for Vancouver's

A carved mask in a tree trunk outside the First Nation village of Yaculta advertises the carving studio of a First Nation artist.

first lieutenant). And it was here that European settlers came 100 years later, establishing a village providing all the essentials of pioneer life: a post office, school, hotels, sawmills and a salmon cannery. Forestry, and gold and copper mining in the northern hills, helped sustain the little settlement. Before Campbell River was settled, "Q" Cove was one of the larger villages and supply centres along the Inside Passage. Today, it is still the commercial hub of the island; its few old cannery buildings around the docks and the busy boat traffic give it an interesting salty air. In summer, the Quadra Island Saturday Farmers' Market is always busy. Just north of town is April Point Resort & Spa, a fashionable holiday place since the 1950s whose boating clientele includes visitors from around the world.

Much of Quadra Island is forested, with some first-growth woodlands still remaining in the north, where a string of lakes and a network of old logging roads encourages exploration. The southern section is more domesticated, and certainly more drivable. The three largest settlements, Quathiaski Cove, Heriot Bay (both with ferry terminals), and the vibrant First Nation community of We-Wai-Kai (formerly called Cape Mudge, or Yuculta), are on the south side of the island.

This island tour starts at Quathiaski Cove. At the top of the ferry road, turn south (right) along Green Road, which descends to a sweeping beach-rimmed bay facing Campbell River across Discovery Passage. Here, We-Wai-Kai village spreads along the shore, clustering around the church and the Nuyumbalees (meaning the "beginning of all legends") Cultural Centre and museum, designed in the shape of a sea snail. Housing a wealth of ceremonial potlatch regalia confiscated and then returned by the Canadian government, the museum is three storeys high with tall house poles rising up from the ground floor to support the roof. Old totems stand at the entrance, along with several boulders carved with ancient petroglyphs, moved here from the shore. The gift shop offers locally made Native arts and crafts, and sometimes artists can be seen at work in the nearby carving shed. Facing the beach is an open-air storytelling arbour, Ah-wah-qwa-dzas ("gathering place"), its roof supported by tribal emblems. Walk along the shore toward the wharf to see a huge decorated cedar canoe and a totem pole lying in the grass.

Bill Reid's design carved on an interior cedar wall of the white clapboard Quadra Island United Church (1913), combines the central

Quadra Island United Church in Yaculta looks like a typical Christian church on the outside. Inside, it sports a cedar wall carved with traditional motifs by artist Bill Reid.

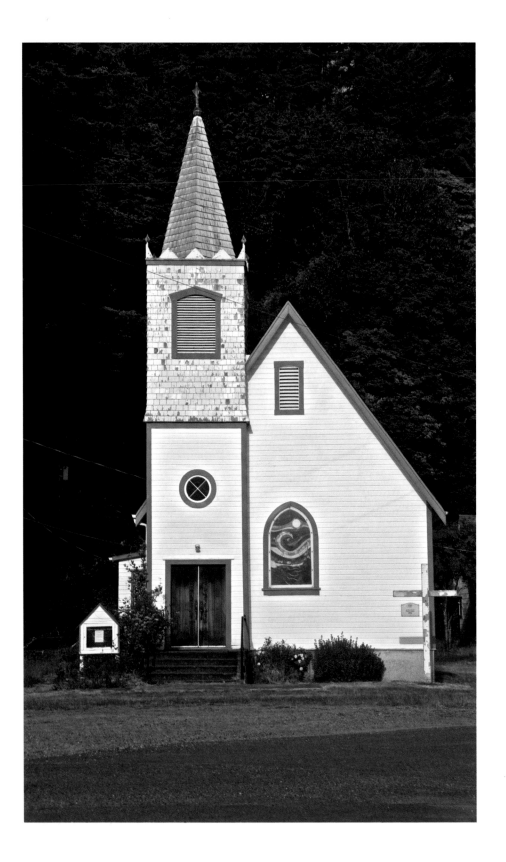

Deck chairs invite lounging outside the Heriot Bay Inn, near the Cortes Island ferry dock.

themes of First Nations and European beliefs: two salmon enclosed in a circle, fish being a symbol of Christianity and the First Nations' staff of life. Missionaries arrived on Quadra Island as early as 1878, but the people at Cape Mudge were the only ones to build a church. The cemetery is interesting, housing both First Nations' and Christian memorials. The oldest grave marker dates from 1890, and the most striking feature is a totem with arms outstretched.

The shore road climbs steeply up onto the bluff, where it joins Cape Mudge Road. Turn right here and head toward the lighthouse via Joyce and Lighthouse roads. The Cape, a strategic spot for navigation through dangerous Discovery Passage, has been home to a lighthouse here since 1898, although today it is fully automated. It is a fine-looking building, spruced up in red and white, with its base in the greenery just above the shingle beach. Watch for herons and other shorebirds stalking the shallows and eagles and osprey in the trees. A short beach walk north from the lighthouse leads to Tsa-Kwa-Luten Lodge, its two-storey lobby beamed in heavy timbers reminiscent of a First Nations big house, an appropriate design, since it is run by the Cape Mudge Band and occupies the site of the old Salish clifftop village. There are artifacts in the lobby, gardens and greenery, excellent views, good sunsets and wonderful food, including some First Nations dishes. On the beach below are about 50 known petroglyphs of ancient origin, some indecipherable and most visible only at low tide. To drive to the lodge, take a west turn off Lighthouse Road. Displayed on the grounds is a mammoth piece of steam-logging equipment known as a donkey.

Detour east along Sutil Road to visit SouthEnd Farm Vineyards, then return to Cape Mudge Road and head north. At the intersection with Quathiaski Cove Road, angle right onto winding

Heriot Bay Road and look for the old graveyard, where many of the island pioneers are buried. A parking lot at the corner of nearby Smith Road is the start of a short trail to the pioneer Haskin Farm and beach access. A short distance beyond, Rebecca Spit throws a protective arm around the outer edge of Drew Harbour. A day-use provincial park, the long sandy spit, crowned with forest, was once a battleground between the Coast Salish and the Kwakwaka'wakw nations, and archaeologists surmise that some of the heaped ridges of sand might indicate old fortifications. One can drive halfway along the two-kilometre spit and then walk along the inner and outer beaches, one with calm water, the other often asplash with huge breakers. For breezy salt-air walks, good birdwatching and great island views, the spit is justifiably popular. Its beaches have long been playgrounds for Quadra Island residents; their May Day celebrations, including a maypole dance, have been held here since 1898. The band-owned We-Wai-Kai campsite at the start of the road provides the only public camping on the island.

Heriot Bay Road runs right to the dock at Quadra's second-largest village, where ferries to Cortes Island start their 45-minute run across Sutil Channel. Near the dock but nicely set back from the water's edge by placid lawns and riotous flower beds is the historic Heriot Bay Inn, an enterprise that has been in the same location here since 1894, though most of the present-day building dates from 1916. The old-fashioned heart of the community, the inn exudes a sense of pioneer friendliness; the gardens leading down to the beach and the fine old maples lining the shore are utterly right in such a setting. There's more to the village near the main road above the harbour: a general store and post office, a smattering of craft shops and a cluster of homes.

The Heriot Bay Inn, the centre of the community, has offered hospitality since 1894, though it has been much renovated. The gardens are always lovely.

The view from the wharf at Yaculta takes in the mountains of Vancouver Island; here, an eagle watches for prey in the kelp beds.

From Heriot Bay, drive north on the island's main highway and meander around Hyacinthe Bay, where a river estuary provides excellent birding. Continue north and consider a short, steep hike up Chinese Mountain for unparalleled views of the island. Then drive the unpaved road through the forest to Granite Bay, a major settlement back in the 1890s, when supplies for the store and hotel were brought in by steamship to a public wharf. Only the wharf and a straggle of abandoned logging and mining machinery along the road (from the 1903 Lucky Jim gold and copper mine) remain, but families are moving in to enjoy a "back-to-the-land" lifestyle. Return to the main road (Village Bay Road) and continue north, where a large section of the thickly forested land, now within a provincial park, is laced with an interconnected chain of lakes, including Village Bay, Mine and Main, providing a popular canoe and kayak route. The road crosses Village Bay Lake and heads north to Surge Narrows, where the northeast bulge of the island almost bumps into Read and Maurelle islands, and the tides between them are fierce. A trail provides good views from the shore at road's end.

Backtrack to the bridge at Village Bay Lake, turn east onto Bold Point Road and follow it to its end. The view of the Breton Islets and across to Read Island are worth the drive. Walk down to a dilapidated wharf, the crumbled relic of the old post office, and a wizened orchard, all that remains of a pioneer farming community begun in 1889 when Moses Ireland, legendary miner, logger, mill owner and freighter, took up a homestead and started a cattle ranch, in addition to running the hotel and post office. Later owners continued to ranch here and shipped their cattle out live to feed logging camps in the area. The post office remained open until supply

163

Folk-art signs point the way to old Whaletown, across the bay from the ferry terminal on Cortes Island.

boats stopped calling at the wharf in the 1950s. Back along the road, look for the sign to Bold Point Farmstay, a working farm and idyllic B & B. Return south the way you came, stopping to explore other side roads in the ferny woods. From Heriot Bay, take West Road, a more direct route into Quathiaski Cove.

For another island experience, take the ferry from Heriot Bay across to Whaletown on Cortes Island, the start of a circular drive that will happily occupy another day. One thing to bear in mind is the ferry schedule: the last return ferry leaves at 5:50 p.m. If you are running on relaxed island time, plan to stay overnight. Cortes is, even today, a sleepy little island, 25 kilometres long and 13 wide. The ferry service began only in 1969, and electricity came to the 400 inhabitants a year later. Its current population has settled at just over 1,000, though this number increases in summer as visitors come to enjoy the relaxed pace of life here. Even so, there are only a few B & Bs, one motel and one government campsite. Advance booking for accommodation is advisable in summer months.

Named in 1793 by Spanish marine surveyor Don Cayetano Valdes after Hernando Cortes, conqueror of Mexico, Cortes Island is a scenic ferry ride from Heriot Bay, around the tip of Rebecca Spit and across Sutil Channel to Whaletown. The original inhabitants of Cortes, the small Klahoose First Nation now based at Squirrel Cove, left a sprinkle of prehistoric pictographs and heaps of shell middens around their old village sites along the shore. Cortes clams, rock oysters, cockles and mussels—all vital traditional food sources for the Klahoose—are still gathered and seeded commercially in island bays.

The first island exposure to European commercialism was a whaling station. In 1869, the Dawson Whaling Company set up shop and conducted their gory business so successfully that, in less than two years, they had almost wiped out the local whale population and the station was closed. Only the name of Whaletown village recalls the era. Later came handloggers and pioneer farmers, the first in 1886, but few of them stayed. The island was just too isolated.

Like Quadra, Cortes Island's northern half is still mostly forested, and the major settlements are in the south, well into the rain shadow of Vancouver Island's mountains. Here, open bluffs support stands of arbutus and juniper, the farthest north on Canada's west coast that these plants will grow.

A day's drive clockwise around the southern half of the island will take in most places of interest. It's good to remember that museums, artists' studios and markets are mostly open only in summer.

The ferry docks on the north side of Whaletown Bay. Drive right at the first intersection, curve south around the deeply indented bay and continue on to Whaletown Road. Where the road angles east, turn right and head toward old Whaletown (follow the hand-painted post office sign), passing the former schoolhouse, now a gallery for the island's many artists, and the old Columbia Mission church of St. John the Baptist. The road ends at the wharf, across the bay from the ferry dock. The colourful old general store that used to sit beside the wharf has been converted to a vacation rental house, but the tiny post office survives, along with an equally tiny village library. Oyster baskets in the bay are visible at low tide.

Return to the intersection and turn right (east) on Whaletown

Fishboats tie up at the Government Wharf near Manson's Landing. The exquisite shell beach and the nearby lagoon make it a popular island destination.

Road, which skirts the edge of Gorge Harbour, a wide, almost landlocked bay dotted with little islands. Open to the sea only through a narrow channel edged by granite cliffs, the slot-like entrance gave the harbour its name. The Native pictographs on the cliffs are visible only from a boat. At the head of the bay are a marina, restaurant, general store and accommodations, all in a grassy, park-like setting.

Whaletown Road meanders northeast to Squirrel Cove, a small community on the island's east side that has kept its commodious general store, which is painted a deep red. Groceries are on the main floor, hardware and marine supplies down below. Adjacent is an arts and crafts shop, and a little farther along the bay, a restaurant whose outdoor patio commands a wonderful view across the strait to the mouth of Desolation Sound. Because of its location, government dock and proximity to a well-stocked store, Squirrel Cove is a favourite anchorage for boaters. On the beach is the wreck of a huge wooden ship, whose hull towers above shellfish-strewn tidelands. Walk along the beach north to Klahoose Village with its white-painted church, keeping a lookout for black oystercatchers, which nest here. And where there are oystercatchers, there are oysters, free for the taking, though some of the tidelands here are privately leased (leases are marked with red concrete blocks). Squirrel Cove hosts the island's Oyster Festival in May.

South from Squirrel Cove, the road heads past Cortes Bay and continues via Bartholomew Road to Manson's, the island's commercial centre, with shops and eateries on the south shore of Hague Lake. The museum and tourist information office are in the old store, surrounded by heritage gardens. South, Sutil Point Road leads to Smelt Bay Provincial Park, with its beachside

campsite. The bay is well named: thousands of silvery smelt still come to spawn in the shallows here. Nearby is the fashionable Hollyhock Educational Retreat Centre (and spa) at the end of Highfield Road. Its restaurant is open to the public, and it has a good art gallery. You can book boat tours from here to tiny Mitlenatch Island Nature Provincial Park, a wildlife preserve known for the largest colony of nesting seabirds—including gulls, cormorants, pigeon guillemots and rhinoceros auklets—in the Strait of Georgia, and for the riotous displays of spring and early summer wildflowers.

North from Manson's is Manson's Landing, where the first island settler, Michael Manson, arrived from Scotland's Shetland Islands in 1886 to start a sheep farm. To stop island predators from decimating his flock, he rowed his sheep to pastures on Mitlenatch Island. Manson also ran a store that was patronized by the local Klahoose. They arrived by canoe and paid for their provisions with dogfish oil. Manson sold the oil to the coal mines at Nanaimo, where it was used to lubricate machinery. Later he ran a steamboat tug for transporting men and freight to logging camps around the coast. The point of land and the deep lagoon it protects are now in Mansons Landing Provincial Park, which is open for the public to collect clams, oysters and other shellfish. The white sand and shell beach is dazzling. Fresh salmon is sometimes available from fishboats tied up at the government dock, and in spring, islands in the lagoon are bright yellow with flowering sedum.

If you have time to spare, there's a fine freshwater swimming beach on nearby Hague Lake, and many former logging roads to explore. Whaletown and the return ferries to Quadra and on to Campbell River are a short drive north along Gorge Harbour Road. ❖

14

SEA LANES TO HISTORY

Many settlements along British Columbia's coast are still accessible only by sea. This is understandable, given the convoluted coastline and the history of European colonization. For the first hundred years, after first contact by Captain James Cook, Europeans conducted their explorations and trading ventures along the sea lanes that connected the wealth of islands and inlets all along the coast from Vancouver Island to the Arctic ice. They arrived by sea and returned by sea and placed only a few frail toeholds along the rough west coast where profits could be made first from the fur trade and later from fishing and logging. Even after railways and roads patched British Columbia to the rest of Canada, the outer coast still remains cut off from the mainstream.

It's hard to imagine just how huge and fragmented this mountainous coastline is, broken up into islands and deep inlets, bays, small coves and promontories—and how most of it is wilderness still—but this land, now so sparsely populated, was once inhabited by several large First Nation tribes. For thousands of years, they lived rich lives on the coastal fringe, and, in their cedar canoes, became intimately connected with the sea, making long journeys to the ocean to fish, hunt whales or sea lions, harvest sea otter pelts, and visit kinsmen on isolated inlets. They moved inland from their saltwater villages to hunt for game and trade, and many of their ancient trails still survive, though many of the people themselves, wiped out by European disease and demoralized by cultural exclusions, have not.

You can travel along the rugged west coast's sea lanes by private boat or on a handful of packet freighters that still carry mail, fresh food and supplies to isolated coastal settlements. Once there were many such boats servicing the canneries, fishing and lumber camps, First Nations villages, lighthouses and mines along the shores. Not many of these boats continue to

Friendly Cove has a Government Wharf and a lighthouse where once stood the first European outpost on the Canadian west coast. The Mowachaht First Nation lives here still in the small village of Yuquot.

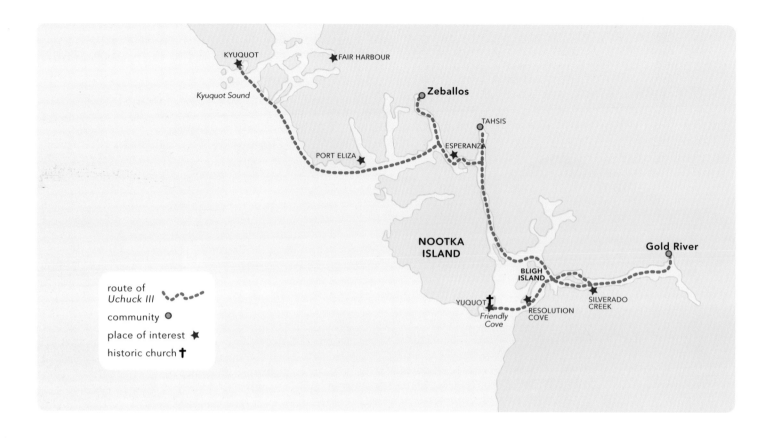

In the map:

KYUQUOT
★ FAIR HARBOUR
Zeballos
Kyuquot Sound
TAHSIS
ESPERANZA
PORT ELIZA

NOOTKA
ISLAND

Gold River

BLIGH
ISLAND

YUQUOT
SILVERADO
CREEK
RESOLUTION
COVE
Friendly
Cove

route of
Uchuck III
community ◉
place of interest ★
historic church ✝

operate, but, luckily, some of the survivors are tourist-friendly and cater to travellers wanting to visit the outposts for hiking, kayaking or just out of curiosity. Given that much of B.C.'s coast is roadless, these voyages by water are fine substitutes for "country roads."

B.C.'s modern history began on an obscure cove on an obscure island at the mouth of an inlet on Vancouver Island's distant west coast, where, nearly 250 years ago, Captain James Cook hauled his ships ashore for repairs. Cook's voyage, the last this great explorer was to make, was primarily a search for the fabled Northwest Passage. With two ships, the *Resolution* and the *Enterprise*, he sailed around the Cape of Good Hope, visited New Zealand, discovered the Hawaiian Islands and then set off across the Pacific, making landfall in Oregon. In March 1778, his battered ships sailed into Nootka Sound and anchored in Resolute Cove (Cook called it Resolution Cove) on Bligh Island. A more sheltered place was nearby, as the Mowachaht in their canoes tried to tell him. "Ichme nutka, nutka," they called, meaning "go round" (into Friendly Cove). Cook thought that Nootka was the name of the people or of the place, and thus the island was put on his map as Nootka Island. Later, Cook took a longboat and followed the local contingent to the village of Yuquot, where Chief Maquinna and his people lived.

The beach at Friendly Cove faces west for great sunsets and island views.

172

Because the people were welcoming and anxious to trade, the place was later named Friendly Cove. Cook raised the Union Jack and claimed the coast for Britain. He stayed for about a month, and his crew traded knives and pieces of metal, mostly for sea otter pelts, furs that were to bring fantastic prices when they were traded in China on the homeward journey. These dense, glossy furs put B.C. on the international trading map. British, Spanish, American and even Russian traders soon learned about the easy profits to be made here, and it wasn't long before the first commercial trader, James Hanna, arrived in 1785—and sailed away with a rich haul of 560 sea otter pelts.

This was the start of 20 years of maritime activity on the west coast during which the local Nuu-chah-nulth (formerly referred to as Nootka) became used to seeing flotillas of ships with tall white sails crowding the harbour, and strange bearded men in longboats. The richness of the fur trade almost precipitated a war when the Spanish tried to claim the land. But Britain's sovereignty over North America's northwest coast was solid—and not only because Cook had made the first landfall. One of the many British traders, James Strange, decided to leave ashore his ship's surgeon, John Mackey, to live with Chief Maquinna and learn the language. Mackey thus became the first British resident in what was to become British Columbia.

In 1788, John Meares, retired from the British Royal Navy, came to Friendly Cove in the ship *Felice* and negotiated with Chief Maquinna for land on which he built a trading post that included living quarters, a storeroom and a workshop. This was the first European building in B.C., and Meares became the first British landowner. When the structure was finished, he built

The Uchuck III *carries freight as well as passengers from Gold River to Friendly Cove, and some stops are made at fish farms along the way.*

A sudden storm blows up from nowhere in the middle of a sunny afternoon in Muchalat Inlet.

a ship, the *Northwest America*, the first to be launched on the coast. An inscription on the cornerstone of the Yuquot church commemorates this historic event.

Despite all of this, in 1789, 11 years after Cook had arrived, the Spanish (under Esteban Martinez) landed at Friendly Cove to claim the land for their king. They seized three British merchant ships, built Fort San Miguel (the only Spanish fort ever to be built in Canada) and a trading post, Santa Cruz de Nuca. They occupied the cove for the next six years. They based their claim on the fact that, four years prior to Cook's landing, Captain Juan Perez and the ship *Santiago* had sailed along the coast, anchored off Estevan Point and traded with the local First Nations. They had not landed. British sovereignty was eventually upheld at the Nootka Convention of 1794, which was signed by captains George Vancouver and Bodega y Quadra, the latter the commander of the Nootka fort. The Spanish withdrew, and the coast was clear for trading to continue. Ironically, by this time sea otters had been hunted almost to extinction. Seal furs became the next preferred trade item, and when they, too, became scarce, whalers moved onto the coast. But at Yuquot, the 20-year flurry of excitement was over, and, after a brief interlude as a fish cannery outpost, Friendly Cove slipped back into isolation and obscurity.

Archaeological investigations show that First Nations have lived at Friendly Cove for at least 4,500 years, and watercolours made by Captain Cook's ship's artist John Webber show many cedar houses, people and boats along the shore. These people were renowned whalers. Yuquot is today almost deserted; only one family remains here year round. The snug harbour, with its large Government Wharf, is overlooked on one side by a high promontory, the former

The Yuquot church beside the old Spanish gardens looks Catholic on the outside but is now a First Nations Cultural Centre. Visitors muster here for orientation and tours.

site of the Spanish fort and also the place where a lighthouse—one of the few manned installations in B.C.—was erected in 1911.

The white Catholic church, built in 1956 to replace the historic 1889 building destroyed by fire, is now used as a cultural centre and shows its traditional allegiance with vividly painted and carved totemic house posts at the doorway and altar. In the choir loft/museum is a collection of drawings made by Spanish crewmen. Two stained glass windows, commemorating the Spanish settlement and the treaty with the British, were gifts from the Spanish government.

In front of the church, where the Spanish once tended garden plots, a flowery meadow slopes down to a beach where a large fallen totem is fast being overwhelmed by a tangle of blackberries. (When totems fall, First Nations people allow them to sink back into the earth.) One house remains in the once-populous village, and one carving shed, where, in summer a carver is often at work. Still, the Mowachaht/Muchalaht people, now dispersed throughout the area, consider Yuquot their home base and return for ceremonies and festivals. A short walk around the beach side of the peninsula leads to rental cabins beside a lake where a small island once housed the tribe's sacred whaling shrine, a structure containing nearly a hundred carved figures of humans and whales and 16 human skulls. The shrine and its contents were carried off by collectors and are now in New York's American Museum of Natural History; the Yuquot villagers await their return.

The whole of Friendly Cove is today a National Historic Site, abutted on the north by Santa-Gertrudis Boca del Infierno Marine Provincial Park. The narrow entrance to the "Mouth of Hell" Bay has fierce reversing tidal rapids, which presumably suggested its colourful name to the Spanish.

Reached only by sea, as in the old days of discovery and trade, Yuquot and Friendly Cove are at the end of one of the great modern sea lanes, down the long, ice-scoured fjord of Muchalat Inlet from the town of Gold River. (The high peak to the west of town is the Golden Hind, named for Sir Francis Drake's little ship, which some historians claim sailed along this coast

and made a landfall in 1579, 200 years before Captain Cook.) Twice a week, on summer Mondays and Saturdays, the working freighter *Uchuck III* makes return day trips to Friendly Cove. This is the easiest way for visitors to connect with this area's early history. It's a 2.5-hour cruise down the inlet, and the boat calls at several fish farms en route. A map shows places along the inlet (Jackfish Bay, Jacklah River, McCurdy Creek, Silverado Creek and Mooyah River) where today there may or may not be something to see—perhaps a fish farm, a logging base, a sports fishing lodge or a campsite. When the salmon are running, several of the inlets might be aswarm with fishboats, but it is, on the whole, still a "great lonely land." At the mouth of Muchalat Inlet, the boat slides down the east side of Bligh Island (named for Cook's navigator, who was later captain of the HMS *Bounty* of mutiny fame), past Resolute Cove and across the mouth of Nootka Sound. It anchors

The church interior houses traditional house posts and some fierce-looking totems beside the former altar.

When totems fall, they are allowed to sink peacefully back into the earth, like this one, almost drowned in greenery beside the Friendly Cove beach.

at the government dock at Yuquot in Friendly Cove, where it stays for a couple of hours or longer before making the return trip. It is indeed a journey into history.

Gold River, the home dock of the *Uchuck III*, is a few kilometres upstream from the head of Muchalat Inlet. It is a new town built to provide housing for a lumber mill at tidewater and a pivotal point in Island transportation: the Nimpkish logging road leads north to Highway 19 at Woss Camp; another unpaved road meanders 64 kilometres northwest to Tahsis, at the head of Tahsis Inlet, while paved Highway 28 connects to the main Island Highway at Campbell River. Along the Tahsis Road lie the Upana Caves, one of the largest and longest limestone cave systems on Vancouver Island. A boardwalk trail leads through the woods and to a viewing platform, but there are no organized tours. Farther along is the Conuma River Fish Hatchery and access to several bays at the head of Tlupana Inlet, home to flocks of trumpeter swans and huge conglomerations of eagles in early winter. Passing Three Sisters Falls and Malaspina Lake, the road reaches the head of Tahsis Inlet, some 30 kilometres almost directly north from Friendly Cove. The village of Tahsis or ("Gateway") has much to interest adventure tourists, including more caves, such as the 7.6-km-long Thanksgiving Cave, as well as fishing, scuba diving, kayaking and wildlife watching.

Tahsis can also be reached from Gold River, perhaps more comfortably, by the *Uchuck III*, which provides once-a-week return trips from September to May, delivering passengers and freight. Other *Uchuck* destinations include summer overnight trips to Zeballos and year-round once-a-week sailings to Kyuquot, another village reached only from the sea and divided by

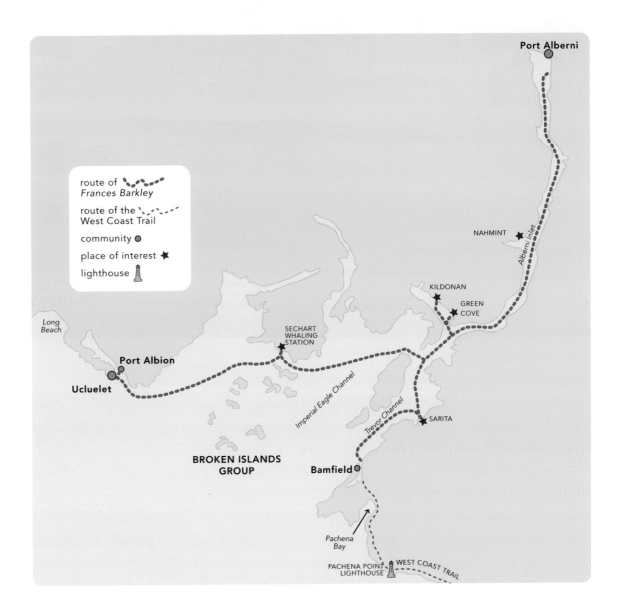

Legend:
- route of *Frances Barkley*
- route of the West Coast Trail
- community
- place of interest
- lighthouse

Port Alberni

Alberni Inlet

NAHMINT

KILDONAN

GREEN COVE

Long Beach

SECHART WHALING STATION

Port Albion

Ucluelet

Imperial Eagle Channel

Trevor Channel

SARITA

BROKEN ISLANDS GROUP

Bamfield

Pachena Bay

PACHENA POINT LIGHTHOUSE   WEST COAST TRAIL

water into two distinct communities. On the Vancouver Island side is the thriving First Nation settlement of Houpsitas, still on its traditional winter home site and a stronghold for Native arts, including finely crafted cedar baskets. Opposite is diminutive Walter's Island (only one kilometre long), first settled by Scandinavian whalers who turned to fishing when the nearby whaling station of Cachalot closed. Here, Walter's Cove is the business district of the combined village of Kyuquot, where the handful of buildings, including small stores, a restaurant and accommodations are linked by "Highway One," a wooden boardwalk and trail. Travel between the two halves of the village is by local water taxi or private boat. With a combined population of around 300, Kyuquot relies heavily on the weekly visits of the *Uchuck* for supplies and transportation.

The only other way to reach the village, apart from seaplane, is by pre-arranged water taxi from Fair Harbour, a long rough drive from Zeballos. Kyuquot, the nearest settlement to Checleset Bay's otter colony and the wilderness park at Brooks Peninsula, is a very popular destination for sports fishermen, kayakers and adventure tourists.

Another extraordinary sea lane runs from Port Alberni, at the head of long skinny Alberni Inlet, down to Bamfield (the north end of the West Coast Trail), then across Imperial Eagle Channel, through the Broken Islands of Barkley Sound to Ucluelet, which sits at the south end of the only stretch of the outer west coast reachable by paved highway. The boat that makes this delectable trip is the *Frances Barkley*, another working packet freighter that calls at several communities en route as needed, including dropping off and picking up kayakers, hikers and other adventurers. The run was previously made by the diminutive *Lady Rose*, built in 1937 and retired in 2007, and destined to spend the rest of her days still afloat, but as a restaurant in Tofino. This little ship, one of the last to serve in the historic Union Steamships Company, had a checkered career, serving in Howe Sound, Vancouver Harbour, the Gulf Islands and North Vancouver Island before transferring to Port Alberni for the Bamfield/Ucluelet mail run. During the Second World War, she carried army and air force personnel, as well as mail and supplies. The operating company of the *Frances Barkley*, Lady Rose Marine Services, still bears the little ship's name.

The *Frances Barkley*, a converted minesweeper built in 1958, was renamed for the young woman who at the age of 17 accompanied her husband, Captain Charles William Barkley, on a

trading voyage to the west coast. Frances, who was educated in a French convent, was the first white woman to visit B.C. and also the first to visit Hawaii and Alaska. William was 26 and had been at sea since he was 11, working for the monopolistic East India Company, but he left this job to invest in a private fur-trading venture in the ship *Loudon*, built in London. He sailed to Ostend, where the ship, for unexplained reasons, acquired a new name: the *Imperial Eagle*, and when it left for Pacific North America, it was under the Austrian flag. Ostend was a lucky port of call for the young entrepreneur. Here he met and married Frances Hornby Trevor, and about a month later, in November 1786, they set sail.

It must have been an astonishing honeymoon trip on a sailing vessel around the world for this sheltered daughter of a clergyman. The *Imperial Eagle*, with Frances the only woman aboard, headed to Brazil, rounded notorious Cape Horn, sailed across the Pacific to Hawaii, and then went northeast directly to Nootka Sound, where the ship anchored in Friendly Cove in June of 1787. Soon after their arrival, a canoe paddled alongside and a man clothed in sea otter skins announced himself as Dr. John Mackey, the man who had been put ashore to live with the Mowachaht and learn their language more than a year before. Captain Barkley took him on board to help with the trading. The *Imperial Eagle* stayed at Friendly Cove for a month, then sailed southeast to explore the coast, where Barkley named several features: Barkley Sound, Frances Island, Hornby Peak, Cape Beale (for the ship's purser) and Williams Point. Then, homeward bound via China to sell his furs, he rediscovered Juan de Fuca Strait. While much of the Frances Barkley story involves Friendly Cove, now served by the *Uchuck III*, it is still most appropriate that the ship bearing her name now brings supplies and tourists to other isolated settlements on the Vancouver Island's west coast.

ABOVE *Travel by boat along the fragmented west coast of Vancouver Island gives a glimpse of the huge expanse of lonely wilderness that still exists here.*

OPPOSITE *Dawn casts a golden glow over the docks and walkways at Sechart Lodge. Kayakers come and go, but for lodge visitors, there is peace and quiet— and the occasional whale, eagle or bear.*

Colourful kayaks lie in wait for discovery trips to the nearby Broken Islands.

From Port Alberni, the *Frances Barkley*, which carries 200 passengers and about a ton of supplies, steams down the inlet past China Creek Marina and calls in, when it has mail and supplies to be dropped off, at Kildonan Post Office, site of a 1903 cannery once employing 500 people and now a tiny settlement for those content to live off the beaten track. The salmon hatchery in San Mateo Bay rears Atlantic salmon for commercial fish farms on the site of another former cannery. Stops are sometimes made at Cheeyah Island or Green Cove to pick up shakes and shingles from a mill or deliver provisions to a tiny general store. Summer homes, logging camps and fishing lodges are also on the call list.

Depending on the day of the week, the *Frances Barkley* continues south to Bamfield, delivering mail and freight at the West Dock before crossing over to the east side of the village to pick up and deliver West Coast Trail hikers and supplies. Twice a week, the ship cuts west around Tzartus Island into Imperial Eagle Channel and stops off at Sechart Whaling Station Lodge (just north of the Broken Islands, a prime destination for kayakers). When the Pacific Whaling Company opened its Sechart station in 1905, it was the first in British Columbia. It stayed in production, under numerous changes of name and ownership, until 1917, when it closed for good after catching and processing only 90 whales that year, down from a high of 474 in 1911. Little is left of the whaling station today, apart from some brick remnants and iron chains and hardware.

The lodge is a comfortably converted lumber-company office that was towed down from Port Alberni to provide a base for kayakers setting off for the Broken Islands, or for travellers just

wanting to stay in one of the places along the coast that are accessible only by sea. Because of the *Frances Barkley* schedule, visitors, unless they are off on a kayak adventure, must stay at Sechart for at least two nights. In summer they can choose to cruise farther, all the way to Ucluelet and back, or to return to Port Alberni by way of Bamfield. Most lodge guests are kayakers, but for others, there are forest trails behind the lodge, rich inter-tidal marine life and stony beaches regularly patrolled by black bears seeking crabs and other delicacies. Sometimes whales come right into the bay.

Another maritime freight service that transports passengers to out-of-the way places operates on the east coast of Vancouver Island from its base at Menzies Bay, just north of Campbell River. Here, the cruises are longer, entailing three- and five-day overnight trips. The *Aurora Explorer* is a landing craft that transports heavy equipment and large freight

Black bears regularly scavenge along the rocky shoreline around Sechart Lodge. They nose the rocks over, looking for small crabs.

RIGHT *Forested shores along the west coast hide the remnants of early settlers—fishermen and loggers. This mossy cabin swathed in rhododendrons lies near Sechart.*

through the Strait of Georgia and into the remote inlets of Johnstone and Queen Charlotte straits. It sails the Inside Passage to the northern tip of Vancouver Island into such places as Toba, Jervis, Knight and Kingcome inlets, and beautiful Desolation Sound. The ship has basic accommodation for 12 passengers and crew and a route and timetable answerable only to the demands of freight deliveries. The scenery in these narrow fjords draped with waterfalls and overhung with glaciers is splendid indeed, and all the ports of call are accessible only from the sea.

A voyage on this and the other working boats gives an entirely different view of life along the British Columbia coast: stormy, austere, lonely but ineffably beautiful, perhaps one of the last places on Earth where one can glimpse a timeless and unsullied wilderness. ❧

OPPOSITE *At low tide, the pristine waters around the Broken Islands provide a look at the intertidal world, including starfish of many colours.*

ACKNOWLEDGEMENTS

PREVIOUS PAGES
Sunrises and sunsets are always beautiful along B.C.'s west coast. Dawn casts a serene glow to the Tofino waterfront.

OPPOSITE *A huge setting sun lights up the clouds at Tofino.*

Some of these journeys appeared in earlier books: **Backroads of British Columbia** and **Country Roads of BC and Alberta**. Farther back still, some were published as articles in early editions of *Western Living* magazine and sections have been recently adapted for *Roadtrips* in *Westworld Magazine*. I have chosen not to include a bibliography. If I were to add one, it would be longer than this entire book, for I have, over the years, read just about everything ever written about B.C. and to mention just a few books would be unfair. I take full responsibility for any mistakes— and hope that you will always find your way as you explore with me the incredible landscapes of this westernmost province.

ALSO BY LIZ BRYAN

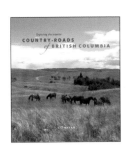

**COUNTRY ROADS
OF BRITISH COLUMBIA**

Exploring the Interior

ISBN 978-1-894974-43-1

**COUNTRY ROADS
OF ALBERTA**

Exploring the
Routes Less Travelled

ISBN 978-1-894974-25-5

THE BUFFALO PEOPLE

Pre-contact Archaeology
on the Canadian Plains

ISBN 978-1-894384-91-9

"It will probably be taken along
on a lot of trips to places such
as Writing-on-Stone and
Head-Smashed-In."

— *CALGARY HERALD*

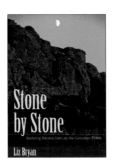

STONE BY STONE

Exploring Ancient
Sites on the
Canadian Plains

ISBN 978-1-894384-90-2

"An excellent introduction
to this fascinating subject."

— *PRAIRIE BOOKS NOW*

LIZ BRYAN is a journalist with an extensive background in magazine editing and publishing. She and her late husband, Jack, co-founded *Western Living* magazine. She is a regular writer for *Westworld Magazine*.